MORE PRAISE FOR
THE MILLION DOLLAR MEDIA REP

"Why can't more Salespeople and Managers get it…it doesn't have to be brain surgery .. it's common sense and courtesy. Michael Guld "gets it." And his book *The Million Dollar Media Rep* is sure to become the standard for broadcasters. The concepts and perspectives of *The Million Dollar Media Rep* will be required reading in successful and client oriented sales departments."
—**Bill Johnstone, President & CEO, Oregon Association of Broadcasters, Past President, National Alliance of State Broadcasters Associations**

"Finally, someone has written a comprehensive "how-to" guide that can launch and sustain a successful broadcast sales career. Michael Guld's comprehensive new book is well grounded in his own success story and covers every square inch of what local broadcast sales reps need to know about themselves and their customers. *The Million Dollar Media Rep* will be standard issue for our television sales recruits. After they read it once, I'm sure they will refer to it often throughout their career. As Michael accurately observes, there are not many college courses for broadcast sales, but the perfect textbook, discussion guide and bibliography is now ready and waiting!"
—**Peter Maroney, VP/ General Manager WTVR-TV, Richmond, VA**

"Michael's experience shines through as he boils down broadcast sales to a user friendly yet comprehensive guide to becoming a successful media seller. *The Million Dollar Media Rep* offers solid, applicable techniques and strategies that can be used by the beginner and seasoned seller alike to advance their career."
—Jackie Weiss, Vice-President/General Manager, Entercom Radio Wichita

"Very practical and down to earth, usable advice, which has been spiced throughout with challenging quotations. Great reading for all media sales personnel!"
—Peter Easter, Executive Director, Virginia Association of Broadcasters

"Finally! A resource the broadcast industry has needed for thirty years. Michael has packaged all the best practices—from how to view the job as a professional to how to make sure broadcast media works for the client –and put them in one place. This book is a platinum investment for new radio and TV sales reps, as well as those veterans who want to crank up their careers! Complete with formulas for advertising ROI, *The Million Dollar Media Rep* content is rich and the read is easy!"
—DJ Mitsch, MCC, Executive Coach, President of the Pyramid Resource Group, Former veteran broadcast VP/General Manager

The
Million Dollar
Media Rep

HOW TO BECOME A TELEVISION AND RADIO SALES SUPERSTAR

MICHAEL GULD

TABLE OF CONTENTS

THE SALES OF ADVERTISING

THE BUSINESS OF ADVERTISING

ACKNOWLEDGEMENTS

In the Acknowledgements of *Built to Last* by James C. Collins and Jerry I. Porras, they refer to Winston Churchill's reflections about writing a book. He states that writing a book goes through five phases. In phase one it is a novelty or a toy, but in phase five it becomes a tyrant ruling your life. Then just when you are about to be reconciled to your servitude, you kill the monster and fling it to the public.

I can absolutely identify! It has been over a year and a half and many hundreds of hours since I first began writing this book. I had no idea what a commitment it would take to get to completion, and at times I wondered if it would ever happen. Early on, I decided not to take any shortcuts because if I was going to do this, I was going to do it right.

I would like to thank Babs Scroggs and Jim Gentry from the Barber Martin Agency for their feedback and perspective; Barry Mitsch for coaching me to completion; Mike Cutchall, DJ Mitsch, and David Friedman for reviewing my work for content; and my editor, Tom Bensman, for painstakingly going through the manuscript and suggesting areas for improvement.

But most of all I would like to thank my family. First, my parents for their continuous support, always giving me the confidence that I could do anything, once I put my mind to it. It was my parents who taught me the importance of values and integrity, and to take a bullet before you compromise your ideals (which I have). To my wife, Natalie, my partner in work and my partner in life, thank you for helping me to chase dreams and allowing me to pull you along for the ride (which can sometimes be bumpy). And to my children Spencer, Stephanie and Justin...I am sure you will be glad once Daddy gets off the laptop. I love you all.

This book is dedicated to the memory of my younger brother Steven, whom I love and miss very much. Steven had a zest for life every day, never worrying about the future. As it turns out...he made the right decision, never missing an opportunity to have fun. It was from Steven that I learned that life is just a game. Play hard. Play to win...but most importantly, always remember to play.

Michael Guld
January 8, 2005

PERSISTENCE...

"Nothing in the world can take the
place of persistence. Talent will not;
nothing is more common than
unsuccessful men with talent. Genius
will not; unrewarded genius is almost
a proverb. Education will not; the
world is full of educated derelicts.
Persistence and determination alone
are omnipotent."

-Calvin Coolidge

The
Million Dollar
Media Rep

HOW TO BECOME A TELEVISION AND RADIO SALES SUPERSTAR

INTRODUCTION

Since getting my first job in media at WSB Radio in Atlanta in 1981, I have worked with most every type of business and encountered just about every type of personality. I have been fortunate to have worked with some of the best people in the business. Martin Sherry, my mentor and first sales manager at WSB Radio and a former Army Ranger in Vietnam, introduced me to media and taught me the importance of mental fortitude in sales. DJ Mitsch showed me the importance of developing a "team," and Michael Corbett opened my eyes to "the real issues of advertising," while Mike Cutchall showed me that honesty and integrity win in the long run.

I have long been a student of the media business. I have been most inspired by the training and teachings of Roy Williams, Don Beveridge, Jim Bleach, and Sheila Kessler. I have also been influenced by the seminars or writings of Jack Trout, Chris Lytle, George Hyde (RAB), Ron Steiner, Paul Weyland, Jim Doyle, Jim Tazerak and Sean Luce. I have benefited from the research that has been available to me from the Radio Advertising Bureau (RAB). It was through a combination of this outside training and my personal experiences that I developed my own way of doing business.

I have worked at top-rated stations, where it is easy to

fall into the belief that you are better than you are. I have learned the most, however, from being at stations that were not high on the ranker radar screen. It was at these places, where sales reps "live or die" based on the results achieved by their clients, that I was forced to get back to the basics of sales and marketing.

The reason that I wrote this book is to share what I would have liked to have known when I was an account rep or what I would have wanted my reps to read in training when I was a sales manager. While there are a number of excellent books available on different aspects of media sales and others on media advertising, to my knowledge there has not been one book that highlighted all aspects of the business the way I wanted them to be presented.

This book is not designed to teach "positioning" one advertising medium over another. It is written to be a "self-improvement" tool that will help any account executive selling radio, television or cable advertising to reach their full potential. While I am not so bold as to believe that my way is the only way, the techniques outlined in this book have worked very well for me and the many reps that I have personally trained in my career.

1. HOW TO GEAR UP FOR THE CHALLENGE

THE WORLD OF MEDIA SALES

In the movie *City Slickers*, Billy Crystal played a burned-out radio salesman going through a mid-life crisis. As a guest speaker for his son's class on career day, he was asked to describe his job. With a lack of passion, he somberly explained, "I sell air." While the on-screen humor was entertaining, the reality is that few sales positions are as difficult as the intangible nature of media sales. All we sell is air…from the air of our sales pitch to the air of our advertiser's message; all we are selling is the "power of persuasion."

On the flip side, few industries evoke as much "passion" as media sales. When asked why they continue to stay in the business after all the challenges and frustrations, many radio and television reps explain, "It's in my blood." Few fields are as interesting and different on a day-to-day basis or as challenging to every skill set we have to offer. Where else can you learn about literally hundreds of different businesses each year? And nothing beats the thrill of exceeding individual sales goals except helping clients exceed *their* sales goals.

Unfortunately, a focused course of study in media sales has not historically been taught or promoted in broadcast journalism schools as much as classes that will help you be a television copywriter or production department manager. Only now are universities beginning to offer limited courses in this area, which I believe presents the greatest opportunity for income and professional growth in broadcasting.

**We are selling air…They are buying results…
If you focus on the results, the air will sell itself.**

SOAR WITH YOUR STRENGTHS

In the book *Soar With Your Strengths,* authors Donald Clifton and Paula Nelson suggest that individuals would be much happier, more professionally fulfilled and ultimately more successful if they are lucky enough (and strategic enough) to choose a profession that they have both a talent for and an interest in. Michael Jordan's talents helped make him a phenomenal basketball player, but he may not have been a world-class physics professor. Likewise, few physics professors have a natural ability to leap from the free throw line to make a slam dunk.

Do your natural talents and interests give you an edge for success in the media sales field? Do you enjoy learning about new businesses? Do you enjoy the sales process? Are you fascinated by the psychology of what makes people do the things they do (and shop where they shop)? Do you have a natural affinity for marketing or a creative edge in advertising? Do you find yourself reading and following media? If so, you have a great chance of being a success in this industry.

The other half of this self analysis is to identify what you do not enjoy doing or what you believe you are not particularly good at. Do you have trouble with organization? Is time management a challenge for you? Have you had difficulty with copywriting? With weaknesses, you can either overcome them (with training, coaching and practice), overcompensate for them (be really good at the other things you do) or delegate to others (i.e., assign tasks to an outside copywriter, personal assistant, etc.)

**Enjoying what you do + Being good at what you do
= SUCCESS**

CHASE A DREAM

Now that you have decided that this field is for you, you should establish some goals. Where do you want to be in one year? In five years? In ten years? What is it that you ultimately aspire to do? When I got back into the radio business as an account executive, I had a 10-year goal to go through all the channels that it took to be a General Manager and ultimately be an owner/partner of a radio station. Eight years (and two moves) later I was a General Manager/Partner of two FM stations in Richmond, Virginia. While the road there took many unexpected turns, the destination was always in sight.

Success is a mindset. You have to be able to visualize it before you can accomplish it. However, conceiving the dream is the easy part. The hard part is devoting yourself to a strategy and executing that strategy to reach your goal. Imagine it...live it...achieve it!

**If you dream it, you can achieve it.
-Walt Disney**

YOU ARE NOT SELLING INDUSTRIAL SCREWS

Few careers have the perceived glamour and glitz of the media business. While on the inside it is easy to get bogged down with the daily pressures and responsibilities, "the biz" always evokes interesting conversations at parties. People like to share their opinions about their favorite program, and they like to hear the inside scoop about their favorite morning show. Since few people ever have the opportunity to meet national celebrities like David Letterman or Ryan Seacrest, local television anchors and morning show DJ's may be the only celebrities that they have a chance to meet in person. Since these local celebrities keep listeners and viewers company in their homes and in their cars day after day, an emotional bond is formed.

It is important to remember that "there is no such thing as a bad day in media sales." No one is dying on the operating table, and few problems cannot be fixed with proper communication. While some days may be better than others, there are rarely boring days. Few careers allow you the opportunity to learn so much about so many different businesses. The more you learn, the more successful you can be!

**Nothing great was ever accomplished without enthusiasm.
-Henry David Thoreau**

SEE OPPORTUNITIES INSTEAD OF OBSTACLES

Your daily perspective as a media rep will affect your daily success (and ultimately your career success). Do you wake up each day and look at work as a "daily chore" or as a "daily challenge?" Do you almost wreck your car trying to write down all the new prospects you see riding down the street or do you only see all the "big" accounts that everyone else has on their account list? Does the thought of walking into a retail business cold to obtain the owner's name for an appointment make you nervous or get you excited? Do you believe that all the good accounts are taken or that there is not enough time in each day to call on all the new accounts that you want to call? While our perceptions may be influenced by others, we mainly see the world through our own eyes.

Nothing can stop the man with the right mental attitude from achieving his goal; nothing on earth can help the man with the wrong mental attitude.
-President Thomas Jefferson

SALES TRAINING DOESN'T WORK

I have been fortunate to have been trained by what I believe are some of the best trainers in the business. While each had his or her own theories and techniques, they all had successful formulas that would yield great results if utilized. However, what I found more often than not with many account executives is that despite the days, or even weeks of training, old habits would reappear once the training book was closed. The new techniques, principles and practical applications preached by the trainers would soon be forgotten after the enthusiasm of the presentation subsided—-and soon, the account executive was no better off than before the training.

As with any sport or any discipline, it is not hearing the

expert tell you the right moves or reading about the strategies in a book that will make a difference in your game. It is all about trying them for yourself and practicing them over and over again until you learn the techniques and they become second nature to you. The same holds true for media sales training: It is how you use information that will make the difference in your performance. If successful, sales training will influence the following...

ATTITUDE – An internal true belief that you can do what it takes to be a success.

KNOWLEDGE – The greater your level of expertise, the greater your confidence.

BEHAVIOR – Establishing good habits with what you know (strategy and execution).

RESULTS – The end result of establishing best practices on the above three.

One of the biggest reasons that salespeople do not succeed is because of inconsistency in behavior and a lack of focus. Always stay focused on your goals and do what it takes to reach them.

**Sales training does not work.
Application and practice of learning does!**

MOTIVATION IS ONLY HEART DEEP

When I first became a sales manager I used to think that I could motivate people. I truly thought that I was good enough to inspire exceptional performance from anyone. I found out the hard way that I was wrong. Not everyone has the same vision, goals and determination. I could motivate in the short run, and I could place consequences for behaviors not followed, but in the end the energy that I exerted was not worth the results I achieved.

I finally realized that I could achieve extraordinary results from extraordinary people by hiring the right kind of people. I began hiring "the heart." When I trained independently motivated individuals who had a burning desire to succeed and who had the right qualities (see "28 Qualities of a Million Dollar Rep" in the next chapter), great success followed, with much less frustration. All I had to do was to give them the tools they needed, point them in the right direction and they were off!

DJ Mitsch, a Master Coach and former radio station GM, says that "motivation is a natural state for people who love what they do." Do you love what you do? If so, you have a much better chance of being a success!

If you work just for the money, you'll never make it, but if you love what you're doing and always put the client first, success will be yours.
-Ray Kroc, Founder of McDonalds™

THE SALES OF ADVERTISING VS. THE BUSINESS OF ADVERTISING

The business of media sales can be broken down into two distinctly different disciplines that involve dramatically different skill sets. These are the "sales of advertising" and the "business of advertising." The "sales of advertising" is little different than other outside sales such as stock or insurance brokerage. It involves the art and discipline of prospecting, preparing, presenting and closing the sale. It also includes the follow-up and service after the sale to build repeat business.

The "sales of advertising" is quite simply all about *our* business, and satisfying the needs and goals of *our* station. On the other hand, the "business of advertising" is what happens once you are actually in the door. At that point, you temporarily take your "sales" hat off and put your "marketing" hat on, focusing on ways to help *their* business grow. While your "sales" approach will get you in the door, it is your "marketing" expertise and creative solutions that will ultimately determine your long-term success.

So, what is more important...the "sales of advertising" or the "business of advertising?" I once hired a former copier salesperson who made more cold calls in a day than I thought was humanly possible. This individual had a drive like no one I had ever seen and an affable personality that helped get her in the door of many businesses. Although she was successful selling packages and closing one-time sales, she did not understand the "business of advertising," and therefore could not survive the attrition of accounts. This person was ultimately more successful selling commodity products, where the sheer volume of presentations is the key to success. This is not a value assessment on who she is, but rather a distinction that shows how an individual's strengths need to match the qualities needed for a specific position.

On the other hand, I once worked with a brilliant marketer who could come up with exceptionally creative marketing campaign ideas, but who lacked the sales skills to develop a sufficient number of prospects to present to. The few people that he saw were easily sold, but the volume was not sufficient to sustain the level of sales needed to be a success. This individual would have been much more successful at a marketing firm or advertising agency, where sales volume is typically not such an issue.

A mastery in both the "sales of advertising" *and* **"the business of advertising" is essential to be successful in media sales.** The skill set and discipline required for the "sales of advertising" ensure that you develop a sufficient number of prospects for presentation, and mastery in the "business of advertising" ensures the success of your client's campaigns and ultimately your career.

The following differentiates the priorities in the "Sales of Advertising" and the "Business of Advertising."

THE SALES OF ADVERTISING SELLING (US)	THE BUSINESS OF ADVERTISING MARKETING (THEM)
Our products	Their products
Our promotions	Their promotions
Our prospects	Their prospects
Our strategy	Their strategy
Our research	Their research
Our competition	Their competition
Our competitive advantage	Their competitive advantage
Our budgets	Their budgets
Our sales	Their sales
Our service	Their service
Our success	Their success

THE
SALES
OF
ADVERTISING

2. HOW TO DEVELOP THE RIGHT SALES PERSPECTIVE

THE OLD DAYS VS. THE NEW WAYS

While extremely entertaining for television, Herb Tarlek, in the 1970's television show *WKRP in Cincinnati* was the stereotypical high–pressure, slick ad salesperson that would give the profession a bad name. In the old days, the media sales process was an arm-twisting psychological battle. It entailed wrestling for buying signs and pouncing on opportunities. The standard close involved laying the proposal in front of the prospect with your pen on top, asking for the order and shutting up, believing that the first to speak would lose.

In the old days you were taught to ask all the right questions, but you had no idea what to do with all the answers. The problem with the old techniques was that prospects could see right through the hard-sell tactics. The perceived manipulation created an offensive-defensive posture between the sales rep and the prospect, with a win/lose end result.

Fortunately, the selling techniques of the old days have been replaced by more pleasant and effective strategies that are based on developing mutually beneficial relationships with clients. The new ways of selling media stress having empathy for a client and showing concern and understanding of the client's unique situation that builds a true trusting partnership, followed up by strategic ideas and solutions to help grow the client's business.

The new media rep tries to diffuse tension by allowing customers to feel more comfortable and to be themselves without the risk of "being sold." For the new media rep"making the month" is of much less concern than building a career. The new media rep understands that by helping clients to make "their" months, the media rep's months will take care of themselves.

Will Turner, President of Dancing Elephants Achievement Group, in Richmond, Virginia, and author of *Six Secrets of Sales Magnets* believes that 21st Century selling needs "sales magnetism" that delivers results without pressure. The premise behind "sales magnetism" is that throughout the selling process, sellers attract those customers that are the best fit without exerting pressure (the key word being "attract").

The following list differentiates the qualities of "The Old Days" and "The New Ways" in media sales:

THE OLD DAYS	THE NEW WAYS
Slick	Sincere
Interesting	Interested
Canned	Customized
Hard close	Hard questions
Great negotiator	Great problem solver
Selling products (commodity)	Selling solutions

**The old ways worked very well in the old days.
Reaching an ever-changing marketplace
requires ever-changing strategies.**

THE SALES "PRODUCT" VS. THE SALES "PROCESS"

When you choose a doctor, what qualities are you looking for? If you are like me, "clinical expertise" and "bedside manner" are both important. The clinical expertise (the product) is essential for accurate diagnosis and treatment of "physical" ailments, but I also seek a doctor who is sensitive to my emotional needs if my child is going through difficult times (the process). I need a physician who will take the time to explain the problem and what is needed, one who is sensitive and empathetic and one that treats my family like people, not just patients.

Every industry has a product (or service) that they sell (or offer) and a process by which the product (or service) is ultimately delivered. In a specialty store, for example, dresses might be the product, but the customer service experience is the process. In the real estate business, every realtor in a given area has equal access to the same inventory of homes, so it all comes down to the process, or the customer experience. Some companies, such as Nordstrom, become known more for their "process" than for their "products."

The product in your business is the commercials on the air. Ultimately, the success of your client's campaign comes down to what is heard, where it is heard and how many times it is heard. However, you will find that there is a lot more that goes into the "process" that will impact greatly on your reputation, your repeat business and, ultimately, your success. Read on!

The difference between an extraordinary player and an ordinary player is that little extra.
-Michael Burks, coach

WHAT MAKES A MILLION DOLLAR MEDIA REP?

When I ask new reps to the business, "Who wants to bill $1,000,000 a year?" there is always a unanimous show of hands. Everyone in media sales *wants* to make a lot of money, just as everyone *wants* to lose weight or *wants* to be in shape. The problem is that there is no commitment to action in *wanting* something. Even *trying* has built-in excuses. The real question is, "Who is committed to apply the discipline, determination and education to bill $1,000,000?" As evidenced by the high turnover rate of media sales people in the first year, the vast majority are not.

My first media sales job was at WSB Radio in Atlanta. As a confident new college grad with an MBA from The University of Georgia, I was ready to take on the radio world in the first 30 days. Martin Sherry, my first mentor and Sales Manager immediately gave me the freedom to "hit the streets" and start making sales. After one week of "getting my teeth kicked in," I crawled into his office one afternoon and said "I need help." He laughed and told me that I was now ready for training. Allowing my early failure was the first step of his training: to show me that all of the other sales people who were making big money and driving nice cars were well-trained professionals who had paid their dues.

As a sales manager I had four broad criteria that I used to hire new media salespeople...talent, determination, attitude and skills. The "talent" may be that great personality that naturally draws people to listen to you or the creativity that enables you to conceptualize exceptional promotional campaigns. "Determination" is that internal drive to succeed and that self motivation to keep going, even on the most difficult days. "Determination" is enhanced by the ability to "visualize" the end result and the ultimate goal. When it comes to "attitudes," people either see the glass half-full or half-empty. Every day is viewed as bringing new opportunities or overcoming new obstacles. The remaining criterion was "skills." Whenever I found someone that fit the first three criteria well, I knew that teaching the skills and training them to sell would be easy.

Some people dream of success, while others wake up and work hard at it.
-Source unknown

28 QUALITIES OF A MILLION DOLLAR MEDIA REP

Do you have what it takes to be a top producer in this field? The 28 character traits listed below are prevalent among the most successful reps. On a scale of 1 (lowest) to 5 (highest) how would you "honestly" rate yourself on each characteristic? With few exceptions, if you rate yourself either a 4 or a 5 on most of the traits, and you have the discipline to learn, practice and execute the skills, you will be a success.

[ ] Self starter	[ ] Adaptable	[ ] Persistent	[ ] Magnetic
[ ] Optimistic	[ ] Flexible	[ ] Persuasive	[ ] Winner
[ ] Passionate	[ ] Responsible	[ ] Dependable	[ ] Successful
[ ] Honest	[ ] Energetic	[ ] Organized	[ ] Goal driven
[ ] Confident	[ ] Ethical	[ ] Creative	[ ] Courageous
[ ] Intelligent	[ ] Accountable	[ ] Trustworthy	[ ] Influential
[ ] Open minded	[ ] Resourceful	[ ] Coachable	[ ] Professional

Sales is part art and part science, part technique and part talent. Internal processors in our brain help us determine what to say. Internal filters help us determine what not to say. Like a swan gracefully gliding through the water, but paddling hard underneath the water to reach its destination, the Million Dollar media rep will work hard to make it look easy.

We are what we repeatedly do. Excellence then, is not an act, but a habit.
-Aristotle

ARE YOU FISHING FOR FOOD OR FISHING FOR FUN?

Sales is a little like fishing. You are either "fishing for food" or "fishing for fun." It is not much fun sitting on the side of a bridge trying to catch the night's dinner. In contrast, when the fish are biting so fast that you can't pull the lines in fast enough, it's fun! It's no longer "fishing," but "catching." Likewise, being in sales is fun when you are at the top of your game and orders are coming in one right after the other. When you are making few sales—-or none—-and you're barely surviving, then it's no fun at all!

What separates the successful fishermen from those who never get a bite? It may have something to do with their skill level, the location where they choose to drop lines, the bait they use and their technique. They also know that if they have more lines in the water, they'll catch more fish.

The same is true with salespeople. Successful salespeople are typically better trained and have superior skills, know where to prospect, and know what to say and do to be a success. They also understand that the more orders they ask for, the more orders they will get.

Take the time to learn the business from the inside out. Understand that it will take time, and your skill level (and ultimately your success) will be enhanced over time. A magical awakening typically happens after being in the business one year. Usually at that time the learning curve begins to level out, the confidence level begins to increase and somehow you just begin to believe that "you get it!"

**You catch bigger fish by fishing with bigger hooks.
So fish with bigger hooks!**

GET BACK ON THE HORSE

Not unlike many sports, sales is a "psychological game." Professional baseball players sometimes have a string of consecutive games where they have a hard time connecting with the ball. NBA players go in and out of having a "shooting touch." Even Tiger Woods has streaks where he is not playing up to his typical game. During their slumps, most would agree that the problem is not "with their hands" but is "with their head." Once you start losing confidence, you start questioning your ability to succeed.

Sales is no different. While you may have some successes under your belt that can be completely attributable to your talent, determination and expertise, if you get a few turndowns, unreceptive responses or dissatisfied customer complaints, it can be immobilizing for some. This "deer in the headlights" reaction to "external" situations can send some people into a downward spiral if they fail to pull themselves back up.

When you go through these periods of self doubt (which at some point you probably will), remember that you are still the same person that was on top of the world with your last success! You did not just forget how to do all the things that got you to where you are today. Get back on the horse. Make the next call. Secure the next appointment. Make the next sale. And when you do, you will be back in the game!

**Success is going from failure to failure
without a loss of enthusiasm.
-Winston Churchill**

3. HOW TO SET GOALS

GOALS ARE DREAMS WITH A DEADLINE

Dreams without an action plan are just that…dreams. Brian Tracy's quote "Goals are dreams with a deadline" is relevant because only when an action plan is put into place will dreams ever have a chance to become a reality. Every gymnast *dreams* of going to the Olympics. Every baseball player *dreams* of hitting the winning home run to win the World Series. Every football player *dreams* of catching the winning touchdown in the Super Bowl. While few athletes will ever realize these dreams, the ones that do committed themselves to a lifelong plan of action to be there.

The first step in turning dreams into reality is to determine your goals (billing, personal income and ultimate position) and put them in writing. Where are you now and where do you want to be each year for the next five years? For the next ten years? What is your ultimate goal?

Every radio and television station has its budgets, which are distributed among the individual sales reps. Station budgets reflect profit expectations for the station. They have nothing to do with your personal income goals. As an account rep, I was always more concerned about achieving a level of billing that would meet my personal income goals, which usually far surpassed those of the company. Therefore, achieving—even over-achieving—station budgets was never a problem.

Once you set a personal income goal, work backwards to a "by-the-month" or even a "by-the-week" view to determine what level of billing is required for you to reach your goal. While the annual goal may seem overwhelming and unattainable at first, a systematic breakdown of short-term goals will help make the improbable seem possible.

While goals do not have to be complicated, they should be **S.M.A.R.T.**

Specific – What exactly do you want to have accomplished? How will you do it?

Measurable – If you can't measure it, you can't manage it. Have trackable goals.

Attainable – If you see a goal as "too" unrealistic, you will not commit to it.

Realistic – Have "do-able" goals that you are willing and able to work to achieve.

Timely – Have a clear target date to reach the goal; build in mini-goal dates.

Company bonuses and incentives for achievement of personal goals are always welcome—-but they cannot be counted on. Self reward can be counted on. Could you justify a new widescreen TV or a weekend getaway to the islands if you reached your annual goal? If not, raise your personal goal a little higher until you can. Post it and go for it!

A man without a goal is like a ship without a rudder.
-Thomas Carlyle - Author

YOU CANNOT MANAGE YOUR SALES

As much as you would like to manage your sales, it cannot be done. All you can manage are your goals, your plans and your monthly, weekly and daily activities to achieve these goals. Sales are the "end result" of a well-conceived strategy and a successful execution.

By increasing their batting average, baseball players know they can help their teams win games. Basketball players monitor their field goal and free throw percentages, as well as their average rebounds and assists per game. Their individual statistics let them know how they are doing and where they can improve.

Just as it is important for our clients to know their traffic count, their closing ratio and their average ticket, we should know ours as well. Only by knowing our baseline statistics and our triggers for growth can we set our strategies to reach new goals.

**If you do not shoot the ball, there is a 100%
chance that you will not score!
-Source unknown**

YOUR TRIGGERS FOR GROWTH

If you have a goal to increase your annual billing by 40% from $300,000 to $420,000 next year, where is it going to come from? What will trigger this growth? How much will come from new business development and how much from increasing the annual expenditures of existing accounts?

There are many different individual triggers that you can

use to grow your business. After setting your baseline statistics, set a goal for growth for the triggers that you decide to use and then determine a strategy to achieve your goal.

The triggers for growth that you should know are as follows:

- The size of your customer base – How many different accounts advertised with you in the last year? How many accounts, on average, do you have on the air each month?

- Your attrition rate – What percentage of your accounts do you lose each year?

- The average number of prospecting calls you make per week (in person and by phone)

- Your prospecting conversion rate – If you make ten cold calls (or visits), how many appointments will you get?

- Your sales conversion rate – If you make ten presentations, how many of them will ultimately result in a sale?

- Your average order – What is the average dollar amount for the contracts you write?

- The average annual spending per account – Considering that some accounts place annual orders and others place single orders, what is the average advertising investment per account per year?

- Your average rate – What is the average commercial rate over all your orders?

- Your average weekly sales – What is the total dollar amount of sales you write each week?

- The number of years each client has been on the air, often called the customer "lifetime" (used to help figure the value of a customer)

- The lifetime value of each customer – To date, what is the total dollar amount that each customer has placed in advertising with you (or with your station)?

- Your referral rate – How many referrals did you receive within the year and what was the total value of those referrals?

Once you know (or can estimate) these statistics, you should set new goals for each. To help estimate activity goals (i.e., the number of prospecting calls per week, conversion rate, etc.) you should start a journal to help you keep track of who you called, the date you called, who gave you an appointment, when you met, if they were sold, the date they were sold and the order amount. This way, you can baseline your current stats, set new growth objectives and monitor improvement. Focusing on the fundamentals will help you achieve your goals.

If you spend all of your time watching the scoreboard, the ball is going to hit you in the face.
-Source Unknown

1) INCREASE THE SIZE OF YOUR CUSTOMER BASE

How many customers did you have on the air last year? If your last year's customer base included 60 different billing accounts that spent an average of $5,000, the $120,000 increase you're shooting for could be accomplished by developing 24 new business accounts (that's just an average of two per month!) over the course of the year (if average billing stays the same). New business development will always be needed, not only to increase the size of the customer base, but also to make up for attrition.

2) DECREASE YOUR ATTRITION RATE

One of the biggest challenges facing broadcasters is attrition. It takes much more in terms of time, energy and expense to "sell" a new account than it does to renew an existing account. Do you know what your attrition rate is from year to year? How many of your advertisers that were on your air two years ago were on again last year? And how many of last year's accounts are on the air this year? For clients who did not renew their accounts, do you know the reason why? Did they not get the results that they were expecting? Were they not satisfied with your level of service? Could anything have been done differently to keep them as a customer? Can anything be done now to bring them back? While new business development is important, retention of existing accounts is paramount for long-term success!

3) INCREASE THE AVERAGE NUMBER OF PROSPECTING CALLS PER WEEK

One of the easiest ways to increase business right away is to make more sales calls. Media sales is still a numbers game. As the old saying goes, "the more calls you make, the luckier you get." This is not to say that quantity is more important than quality. They are both important. The better the quality of the prospect, the better the conversion rate to get an appointment (and ultimately a sale).

4) INCREASE YOUR PROSPECTING CONVERSION RATE

Your prospecting conversion rate will probably increase naturally as you gain experience. There is a difference in the confidence level that a seasoned ten-year rep has relative to that of a new rep that is just starting out. That being said, there are prospecting strategies (who to call) and there is sales training (what to say) that can dramatically increase your odds of getting an appointment regardless of your experience level.

5) INCREASE YOUR SALES CONVERSION RATE

What if you could go from selling one of every five prospects you present to selling two or three out of every five? What can be done to increase your probabilities? Mastering "the sales of advertising" as well as "the business of advertising" will increase your closing rate.

6) INCREASE YOUR AVERAGE ORDER

This is more of a general measure to give you an idea of how hard you are working for every order. It obviously makes sense that if your average order is $1,500, increasing the average order to $3,000 would either make you more money or save you more time (to work on new orders).

As with any business, some orders will be large, while others will be small, but your focus should be on the average order. To determine your average order, take the total dollar amount of sales for the last year (or another period of time) and divide that number by the number of sales made (orders written) over that same period of time.

EXAMPLE:	
Annual Sales:	**$300,000**
Number of sales (orders written):	**200**
Average sale:	**$1,500**

If you are just starting out and do not know what your average ticket will be, you can get station averages or determine your own goals.

7) INCREASE YOUR AVERAGE ANNUAL SPENDING PER ACCOUNT

Most media professionals and advertising agency executives understand the need for domination and frequency, as well as consistency to increase the probability of success for an advertising campaign. Therefore, if a client's ad schedule is placed effectively and the message is compelling, suggesting an increase in the advertising budget is not just self serving for you, but a good business decision for your client as well.

If the average advertising investment per account were to be increased by just $2,000 per year (from $5,000 per account to $7,000 per account), the $120,000 increase in billing that you are seeking could be met by keeping to the same baseline number of 60 billing accounts.

There are at least three ways for you to help increase the average annual spending per account:

A) SUGGEST AN INCREASE IN THE AVERAGE MONTHLY ADVERTISING INVESTMENT

The more success you have with customers to back-up your earlier claims regarding the effectiveness of your medium, the appropriateness of your station, the service you will deliver and the results you will get, the better the probability that your suggestion will be positively received. Many advertisers who are working on tight budgets do not advertise every week, but they should. Unless a client is only advertising during "sale" periods, it is always recommended to advertise every week to keep the consistency of a campaign going, and to remain at "top of mind." Other advertisers who have chosen limited days (vertical scheduling) or limited shows or dayparts (horizontal scheduling) may benefit by the expanded reach of widening the scheduling. Adding a spot a day to "Live with Regis and Kelly" will bring a new market to a schedule that is already hitting "The Today Show" each day. Adding midday spots to a schedule that is already dominating morning drive will do the same.

B) SUGGEST INCREASING THE DURATION OF THE SCHEDULE

Everyone has a story of the prospect that says they "tried advertising for a few weeks but it did not work." Even today you probably find that the majority of your account base is made up of "periodic" advertisers, with limited consistency on your station. An integral part of increasing the annual spending per account is to show your clients the benefits of signing annual contracts. Possible selling points include…

1. It takes time to break through the clutter to brand your company (share of mind).

2. It takes time to motivate a change in behavior (share of time).

3. People forget about you. (Out of sight – Out of mind).

4. Future buyers" will one day be "now buyers."

For you the benefits of getting your clients to sign long-term contracts are as follows:

1. It increases your base billing.

2. It reduces the amount of time required to go back to "resell" the account.

3. Once the order is on the books, the client feels "pre-committed," making it more difficult for other media salespeople to try to take away your budget.

4. The "reselling" time formerly spent on this customer can now be spent developing new business.

C) INCREASE THE AVERAGE RATES PER CLIENT

Most clients understand that with limited inventory, rates will have to go up as demand for the station increases. However, getting existing clients to buy in to a rate increase will only be accomplished once value has been established for the station and for you as a rep and only if the client received a perceived return on their investment.

If you sell an average of 6,000 units a year ($300,000 annual billing/$50 average rate), an increase of even $5 per commercial unit would produce an additional $30,000 in annual billing. If your average commission rate is 10%, you could give yourself a $3,000 raise by an incremental increase in rates alone.

8) INCREASE YOUR AVERAGE WEEKLY SALES

Establishing weekly billing goals (both individually and for the station) can help to keep annual goals on track. When annual and monthly budgets are broken down into these bite-size chunks, the numbers do not seem quite as overwhelming.

If your average weekly billing (orders written) last year was just over $5,700 to achieve $300,000 for the year, what would your weekly goal need to be for the next year to achieve $420,000 in billing? If you are counting on an estimated $70,000 in annuals to be placed before the year's end, that leaves $350,000 to be made up in billing throughout the year. If your goal is to make your budget by the end of November, your goal should be to write a minimum of $7,300 per week for 48 weeks, regardless of the months the dollars actually fall. The weekly billing could come from one $7,300 annual or from four $1,825 orders. Your weekly plans should put you in a position to reach these weekly goals. If they do not, you will be destined to play catch-up to make your budgets.

9) INCREASE THE LIFETIME OF YOUR CUSTOMER

What would be the difference in your billing if you could increase the lifetime of each of your customers from one year to three years? If they are getting the results they expected, why would they not stay with you? Understand that there are many competing sellers in your medium as well as representatives from newspapers, direct mail, billboards, yellow pages and the internet making a strategy *today* to take away your dollars tomorrow. Therefore, it is imperative that you know your clients like you have never known them before; service your clients like they have never been serviced before; and, most importantly, help them grow their businesses to heights that they never imagined possible before, and they will be customers for life.

10) INCREASE YOUR REFERRAL RATE

Insurance agents and stockbrokers have been pushing their clients for personal referrals for years with great success. This is one of the most powerful ways to build your business, yet few people in our industry ever ask for them. Your clients are all involved in clubs and professional organizations where they interact with business owners and corporate senior managers. If every one of your successful clients was to give you the names of (or, better yet, personal introductions to) just three business contacts, imagine what a difference it could make in your business.

4. HOW TO PROSPECT

HUNTERS AND SKINNERS

There is a big difference between selling direct accounts and selling agency accounts. They involve different skill sets and different training. Years ago, Jim Bleech, a corporate trainer in Jacksonville, Florida, first exposed me to the hunter/skinner analogy. Like a hunter, your dealings with direct accounts are primarily "proactive," or creating opportunity. As with hunters, you eat what you kill. With ad agencies, you operate primarily in a "reactive" mode, responding to opportunities and taking care of the business that comes your way (skinners).

While everyone always considers agency accounts to be the "prime accounts," you will never have control over your destiny if you are too heavily agency dependent. In servicing agencies, you are subject to agency account transitions and to decreasing or disappearing budgets as they are redistributed to other media. You will also be affected by your own ratings fluctuations, which at the very least could affect your rates (and total dollars of the buy) and at worst may eliminate you from a buy if you become too inefficient.

For the most part, the agency buy is a zero-sum game. There are usually finite budgets (Gross Rating Points) allocated to a specific medium, so the only way that you will increase your dollars (your share) is by taking away from someone else's dollars (their share). The challenge is that all your competitors are also positioning for increases over last year's spending and increases in share.

In contrast, direct accounts have much more flexibility in the medium they choose and the budgets they allocate (opportunity driven). As with hunters, the big challenge working with direct accounts is identifying the best accounts with the greatest opportunity. Once you have identified the accounts you will pursue, you should be able to answer four questions from their perspective:

1) **Why advertise?**

2) **Why advertise on your medium?**

3) **Why advertise on your station?**

4) **Why work with you?**

For direct accounts, you are typically working with the owner of the business or the person directly responsible for the results. In many cases, your station may be the only station bought, so the responsibility falls directly on you to deliver the anticipated results. Therefore, the direct accounts are looking for you to be the expert in scheduling, creative, and promotions.

Great hunters never have to worry about going hungry.

JUST BECAUSE THE DOORS ARE OPEN DOES NOT MEAN THE BUSINESS IS A QUALIFIED PROSPECT

Not every business is a broadcast media prospect. Many businesses simply may not be appropriate for your station or may not have a large enough drawing radius or enough locations to make advertising with you cost efficient. This is not to say that they can't be sold one time. However, an unsuccessful initial campaign will not promote the good will that might be needed at some future time after their business has grown and truly becomes a viable prospect.

As a general rule, the larger the potential purchase the larger the potential drawing radius. The average person may be willing to drive anywhere in the market or even outside the market to purchase a new car. Therefore, a single dealership can get a return on their investment with broadcast advertising. Conversely, a neighborhood video store with a two-mile drawing radius and low average ticket would fair much better using direct mail or a zoned newspaper run. Recommending the appropriate advertising vehicle will pay dividends as this account adds multiple locations and finds that they can benefit from your services.

Factors to consider when prospecting:

- Multiple locations – Does the client have enough locations to spread their advertising investment?

- Average ticket/profit margin – Is the average ticket high enough to provide a return on investment (ROI)?

- Traffic count – If the average ticket is low, is there a

high enough traffic count to still achieve a ROI?

- Drawing radius – Is the drawing radius large enough to benefit by broadcast advertising?

- Demographic profile of the client – Does a typical customer profile fit into your demographic target (age/sex/race)?

- Qualitative profile – Do you do well with buyers or users of your client's products or services?

**You never stumble across a good account
unless you are walking.**

PRIORITIZE YOUR ACCOUNTS AND PROSPECTS

As stated before, time is your most precious asset. Every time you pick up the phone to call a prospect or a client, there is an "opportunity cost" of not calling another prospect or client. The two variables to consider are "potential value" over a period of time (month, year or lifetime) and "probability of sale." For example, Advertiser A, who spends a significant amount on other media (newspaper, television, radio or billboards) may have a significant "potential value" over the course of a year if sold. However, the "probability of sale" may be low due to a bias against your medium or because of a former bad experience with your station. Advertiser B may be a referral from an existing client, with a lower potential value, but a much higher probability of sale. Here is one way to prioritize your target accounts.

EXAMPLE:

POTENTIAL VALUE (YEARLY)	X PROBABILITY OF SALE	= NET PROJECTION
ADVERTISER $50,000	X 10% =	$5,000
ADVERTISER B $10,000	X 75% =	$7,500

The "Net Projection" is $5,000 for Advertiser A and $7,500 for Advertiser B, resulting in a $2,500 "opportunity cost" of working with Advertiser A over Advertiser B.

Does this mean that working with Advertiser A is not worthwhile? Not necessarily. It all depends on the "Net Projection" of other potential prospects. To determine the priority of an account or prospect, project the "Potential Value," "Probability of Sale" and "Net Projection" of each of the accounts on your list. Next, rank your accounts from the highest to the lowest "Net Projection." The goal is to work your best prospects first. You may never get to the accounts on the bottom of your list.

The difference between working with good prospects and great prospects is the difference between having a good year and having a great year.

USE YOUR ACCOUNT LIST
AS THE ROADMAP TO YOUR GOAL

A spreadsheet program can be useful in tracking and prioritizing your accounts and prospects. Along with the previous projections, set up as a combination account/prospect list that can include a location code, contact name(s), telephone numbers and a brief description of your next step.

LOCATION	ACCOUNT	GOAL	% PROB	NET PROJ	STATUS/NEXT STEP	TEL #
Westend	Westend Motors	$20,000	25%	$5,000	Contact GM in Sept.	445-5555
Westend	Westend Jewelry	$10,000	75%	$7,500	Meet in Sept. to write	445-5151
Westend	Computers Etc.	$15,000	50%	$7,500	Present DM in Sept.	445-1212
Downtown	Lottery	$25,000	75%	$18,750	Meet w/ agency in Sept.	888-4545
TOTAL		$70,000		$38,750		

By totaling the "NET PROJECTION," and adding to the business that you currently have on the books, you can see if you are on track for making your annual goal. I call this a "gap analysis." If you do not see yourself reaching your projection, you know that you need to add more accounts to your existing pipeline, increase the "goal" (amounts presented) or increase the "probability of sale" for the accounts/prospects that you pitch. More than likely, it will be a combination of the three.

In most broadcast markets, the distance of potential travel from appointment to appointment is huge. Therefore, you can make the most of your time by clustering your accounts and prospects by region (e.g., downtown, West end, South side, etc.). Schedule your appointments back-to-back by region to maximize your time in the area. Using the location code, you can sort your account data based on geographic territory, making it easier to cluster-schedule. During down time between appointments, drop by your other clients in the area to make appointments for a future day or prospect the region for new clients.

Setting a goal is not the main thing. It is deciding how you will go about achieving it and staying with the plan.
-Tom Landry, legendary Dallas Cowboys coach

EVERY OPPORUNITY HAS A COST

There is a finance term called "opportunity cost" that refers to the lost revenue opportunity of choosing one investment over another. If Investment A will produce a projected 4% return on investment and Investment B is expected to provide a return of 10% on an equal investment, the "opportunity cost" of choosing Investment A over Investment B is 6%.

We have opportunity costs in our business every day. With limited commercial inventory, there is a potential opportunity cost of selling our air time short (selling out), while others would pay more. But for you personally the opportunity cost of prospecting and presenting to a potential $1,000 account as opposed to another potential $10,000 account is $9,000. Maximize your opportunities with your most profitable potential accounts first!

Opportunities are never lost; they are taken by others.
-Source unknown

THEY'RE NOT WORTH MY TIME!

One of the most difficult things for media reps to do is to "disqualify" prospects and to release current accounts from your account list (even if they are billing). It's not always true that the bigger the account list, the greater the billing. By concentrating on fewer accounts and forging deeper relationships, you will probably find more success than casting a wide net with one pass. Concentrating on certain geographic territories may save you more time, and becoming a category specialist may increase your effectiveness in an area of expertise.

How do you know when it is time to terminate a relationship with a current billing account? Some accounts create more stress than they are worth in billing. Problem accounts that are constant emotional drains can zap your energy and diminish your effectiveness in other areas. A good way to determine the cost/benefit ratio of an account is to figure what the value of your time is worth, note how much time you are spending on each account and compare this with the amount you are making on each account.

If you are making $50,000 per year (or that is your goal), your rate (assuming a 40-hour work week) is $24 per hour. If a problem account billing $1,500 per month is netting you $225 per month in commissions and you are spending an average of fifteen difficult hours per month to service that account, you are only making $15 per hour, or less than two-thirds of your average rate. Your time would be better spent on more profitable accounts.

Don't be afraid to fire a bad account.
Be afraid of keeping bad accounts.

PRINT PROSPECTS

Newspapers are by far the biggest players in the print advertising world, capturing the lion's share of all advertising dollars in just about every market. With demographic changes and new media competition, circulation continues to decline (penetration percentages) while column-inch advertising rates continue to increase.

While newspapers continue to sell the idea that "bigger is better," even their own research by the Starch division of Roper Starch Worldwide paints a different picture. The Starch Report scores show that when ad size is reduced from a full page to a half page, the percentage of those readers "noting" the ad drops from 42% to 34%. By reducing the ad size from a half page to a quarter of a page, the number "noting" the ad drops to 26%. This represents a nominal drop but the cost can decrease by as much as 50%. Even an eighth of a page "noting" of 23% represents only a minimal decline from the quarter-page figure.

Print is a "price and item" medium. It can be very effective featuring merchandise during sale periods for the "now buyer." If you are in the market for a new television, in addition to visiting the "top of mind" retailer that you know from broadcast advertising, you may be inclined to check the newspaper to see what is on sale. However, it usually does not matter if the television is featured in a full-page ad or in an ad a fraction of that size—you will probably seek to find all ads that fit what you are looking for.

What's important to note is that consumers not in the market for a new television will probably not see an ad promoting these products. In fact, you could test (diplomatically, of course) your prospects who are sold on print by asking them the following questions. Do they get a newspaper every day? Do they read the newspaper every day? Do they remember any ads from the day? What did the ads say (to the best that they can remember)? While an estimated 50% may subscribe to a newspaper and read a portion of the paper every day, very few can recall specific ads and the associated copy.

Another point to make is that newspaper is reaching an increasingly older demographic. The baby boomer generation counted on newspapers for all of their news and entertainment, while the Generation X and Generation Y demographic will first turn to their computers to get informed on what's going on locally and around the world.

So, why would a newspaper advertiser be sold on broadcast advertising? Unlike newspaper, radio and television can influence emotions through creative imagery, making them more "motivational media." An audio/visual description of an island getaway may influence that burned-out businessman to take that much-needed vacation.

In addition, broadcast advertising can produce a better long-term return on investment by reaching not only the "now buyer," but also by implanting an impression that will have a long-term influence on a "future buyer," who may one day have a need for the product or service advertised.

Research your newspaper's demographics and trends in circulation and pricing.

QUALITATIVE PROSPECTING

If you have access to qualitative research, you will be able to review higher indexing categories that have a greater propensity to view your programs or listen to your station relative to other stations in the market. For example, if your station indexes at 150% for people who "plan on buying a Ford truck in the next 12 months," your listeners/viewers are 50% more likely to buy a Ford truck than the average resident in your market. If another station being considered indexes at 80%, their listeners/viewers are 20% less likely to be a Ford buyer in the next year than the average market resident.

Prospecting higher indexing account categories not only may make it easier to position yourself in the selling process, but also will increase the likelihood of campaign success. On the other side, if there are jewelry stores that do not index as well for your station, but are not on your air, you could make a case that your viewers or listeners may not be as likely to shop at their store because they have not been invited. You could claim that by advertising on your station, they could improve their business by reaching a new clientele.

**Maximize your opportunities for success
by targeting prospects "most likely" to be clients.**

"TIS THE SEASON" PROSPECTING

Everyone knows that the Christmas season is the biggest selling season for most retailers. Jewelers typically garner up to 23% of their annual sales in December. However, for many other broadcast advertiser categories, the "big season" may be at other times of the year. For instance, lawn and garden centers experience their highest sales in the spring and summer, as do theme parks. Most industries have seasonal fluctuations and understandably prefer to market more heavily just prior to and during their peak seasons. If you are contacting these companies in their busy season, it is probably too late. By this time, their budget will have been long spent and they will be too busy to meet with you.

The Radio Advertising Bureau (RAB) has a chart that shows the average monthly sales percentage for major broadcast advertiser categories. It is best to prospect at least six months in advance of the peak season to find out when their advertising planning begins. Working ahead of the demand curve will pay big dividends.

It's always a "holiday season" for some clients.

NEW BUSINESS DEVELOPMENT CATEGORIES

When it comes to prospecting there are literally thousands of potential advertising clients representing a wide range of industries. One of the best ways to prospect for your individual station is to review a list of your advertisers, separated by category. Look for major spending categories and try to identify companies within those categories that are not on your air (and not currently being worked).

Typically, the major broadcast categories include...

AUTOMOTIVE: At most media outlets, a disproportionate share of advertising revenue will come from the automotive sector. It's not that the category is not appropriate or that the business is not appreciated—it's just that the risk of an automotive downturn could have disastrous billing effects on a station's revenue. That being said, automotive still works extremely well in broadcast advertising. The major challenge is creating a commercial that stands out from all the others. In addition to the retail side, there may be potential co-op advertising dollars on the backside (service and parts) that have not been allocated.

CONSUMER PRODUCTS: Television and radio create images and build brands. Whether it's through the animated Budweiser frog, the shadowy dancing silhouettes of the ipod commercial, or the familiar music and folksy sound of Tom Bodett promoting Motel 6, broadcast media moves people to make specific product and service choices.

RETAIL: A billboard I once saw read "A strange thing happens when you don't advertise...nothing!" Retail space is very expensive and most retailers can no longer depend on adjacent tenants to provide the foot traffic to build their business. Therefore, traditional retail accounts that sell everything from jewelry to furniture to clothing can benefit by promoting their services on television or radio. The previously mentioned criteria (i.e., number of locations, average ticket, etc.) will determine the potential benefit.

CO-OP: Manufacturers provide advertising dollars to retailers to help promote their products. The dollars available are usually time sensitive (will expire) and usually cover a percentage of the advertising schedule based on purchases. Co-op advertising dollars may be used to promote an individual account or may be pooled to create a dealer group program.

SERVICES: The retail storefronts at major shopping centers and on major thoroughfares are being prospected by members of every advertising medium many times a day. However, behind this retail "front line" lie office parks with many businesses that do not rely on foot traffic but still need call traffic. Businesses that provide services are getting increasingly competitive and increasingly aggressive in marketing to differentiate their benefits. Services such as mortgage companies, financial planners, attorneys and even the medical community (dentistry, plastic surgery, etc.), that once thought of mass advertising as taboo are now making significant investments in television and radio.

RECRUITMENT ADVERTISING: Chris Stonick has helped create the new industry of recruitment advertising for many broadcasters. Companies have found that the quality of the applicants who respond to radio and television ads are usually superior to that of unemployed people who search the classifieds in the newspaper. The broadcast message is like the voice of a headhunter being received by gainfully employed prospects (as well as by their friends and family). The target prospect is usually in Human Resources, and therefore is someone who is not barraged by all the media sellers every day. In addition, Chris's recommended Sunday, Monday and Tuesday schedules are cost effective for clients and do not put as much pressure on later week inventory.

BUSINESS TO BUSINESS – Business owners and business decision makers watch television and listen to the radio. Targeted campaigns to reach them can be very effective.

EVENT MARKETING – The broadcasting industry has for years been used to promote other people's events and concerts. One day the industry woke up and realized that it had the power (and the inventory) to generate additional revenue from ticket sales and sponsorships.

CAUSE MARKETING – Now more than ever before, companies are aligning themselves with community events, community causes and with local and national charities. While they truly want to make a difference, they also know that enhancing their "do good" image in the community is good for business. McDonald's has the Ronald McDonald House; Wal-Mart promotes their "Teachers of the Year" contributions, and Target makes charitable donations from their profits. Local sponsors are also seeking ways to make a difference, and you can help them promote their causes.

All the good accounts are taken!
-A common myth

5. HOW TO DEVELOP YOUR PROSPECTS INTO CLIENTS

KNOW YOUR MEDIUM AND KNOW YOUR COMPETITION

The Television Advertising Bureau (www.tvb.org), The Radio Advertising Bureau (www.rab.com), and The Cabletelevision Advertising Bureau (www.onetvworld.org) are tremendous resources for understanding the benefits of these media, as well as for providing marketing ideas through previous success stories. Information is also available from these bureaus on competitive media. Now more than ever before, our competitive threats are coming from new technology that is specifically targeted to consumers who want fewer (or no) commercial interruptions.

On the radio front, satellite radio and internet radio are the greatest potential threats. Penetration levels will continue to increase for satellite radio as the automobile manufacturers (who are big investors in XM and Sirius) continue to add the hardware in their new models and to offer special satellite sign-up deals to people buying new cars. The Apple ipod and other portable listening devices also have the potential to erode listenership, especially with younger listeners.

On the television front, satellite television is continuing to encroach television viewership. DVD's, personal video recorders and home computers bring added competition for the eyes of our viewers. In addition, advertisers are seeking alternative ways to get their products front and center through "product placement" in movies and television as well as through "advergames," or the placement of consumer products in video games.

Even with all the new competition, television and radio remain by far the dominant broadcast media offering great opportunities for you and your clients. While it is never a good idea to waste your precious time positioning all of the other media or members of your own media, it is advisable to be informed and know the strengths and weaknesses of each. You never know when you will need to respond to questions raised by your clients.

Know your business to grow your business.

GETTING THE APPOINTMENT

Improving your "prospecting conversion rate" (*appointments made* in comparison to *contacts made*) can have a dramatic effect on your income as well as on how hard you have to work to make your target income. Getting the first appointment for the opportunity to present your marketing services is part science (technique, strategy, prospect hit list, etc.), part art (communication skills, personality, attitude, etc.) and part luck (being in the right place at the right time).

By and large, the more talented a person is in communicating the benefits of his or her marketing services, the greater the prospecting conversion rate. The following tips may help you increase your probability of getting those appointments.

PROSPECT WISELY – The better the target prospects, the better the results

RESEARCH YOUR PROSPECT – Learn more about the challenges and opportunities of the industry and the company. Go online and do internet searches for articles. Go to the RAB (www.rab.com), the TVB (www.tvb.org) or the CAB (onetv-world.org) for research and success stories.

SEED YOUR PROSPECT BEFORE MAKING THE CALL - Prepare a series of letters and information pieces sharing pertinent findings that your prospect may find useful. This helps build credibility and shows that you care about their business and are willing to work hard to help uncover new ways to help their business grow.

DO A PHYSICAL SURVEY – What is your first impression when you walk in the door? How is the selection? Is it well merchandised? How responsive is the sales team? How would you rate the overall customer experience?

DO AN INTERNAL SURVEY - Interview managers, employees and customers to learn about a business from a cross-section of valuable perspectives. You may hear different stories than you will from an owner.

DECIDE ON THE BEST WAY TO MAKE THE CALL - Each of the following options for making the call has its own advantages and disadvantages.

By Phone - Some media sales professionals prefer to initiate prospecting calls by phone. The advantage is that you can make more prospecting calls per day. The main disadvantage is that the conversion rate will probably be lower, given that you are one of hundreds of "invisible" vendors "perceived" to be peddling their services. Phone calls can be easily screened to thwart the efforts of sales people.

In Person – Although you never want to try to secure an unannounced appointment on the spot, the conversion rate of getting an appointment is typically higher when you show up in person. A well-dressed personable media rep may have an easier time talking to a business owner by simply dropping by, or at the very least, meeting an "inside coach" who can help gain access to the decision maker for an initial appointment.

E-mail – More and more communication is being conducted via e-mail. The advantage of e-mail is that it is usually not screened, going directly to your prospect. In addition, there may be times when it is difficult to get a return phone call. However, email may provide an option to get a quick reply. On the negative side, email can be more impersonal, since you are not being seen or heard. It makes it easier for a prospect to turn you down without even an introduction. Always leave yourself open to call back in the event that you do not get a reply.

Most importantly, be yourself! You don't need (and don't want) a canned sales pitch that is difficult to keep flowing amidst diversions and interruptions. However, you do want to have a strategy in mind, and you should be able to articulate an "elevator pitch," a fifteen- to thirty-second summary of who you are and how you can help. It may be helpful to write out a list of potential talking points first (i.e., why advertise? why your medium? why your station? why work with you?).

The more passionate you are about what you do and the more confident you are in communicating your abilities, the more effective you will be in transferring this confidence to others. Experience will help you gain confidence. Also, the ability to share success stories of others you have helped in similar industries will help build your credibility and promote interest from your prospect.

A little customized research also may help to get an appointment with a business owner or decision maker. A rep that I was working with was having a hard time getting an appointment with the owner of a successful, high-end dry cleaning business. I suggested doing research on the company by interviewing its customers (e.g., why they take their clothes to these cleaners; why they switched from another cleaner, areas to improve, etc.). When it comes to trying to get an appointment, you have a little better chance when you can introduce yourself, state that you have interviewed fifteen customers and would like to share your findings, and reveal that you have identified some ways to use this information to help increase their sales.

The more people you call, the luckier you get.

YOU NEVER HAVE A SECOND CHANCE TO MAKE A FIRST IMPRESSION

Year's ago John T. Malloy wrote and published a book called *Dress for Success*. In it he described research that showed that people form their first impression of you based on the way you look and the way you dress, and they then treat you accordingly. If you portray an image of success, people will perceive a greater confidence level in your abilities, and will therefore be more likely to want to work with you.

This theory has a deep basis in human nature. Why is it that I will reflexively step on a big black bug in our house in a second, but if a few ladybugs make their way into our living space, I will carefully cup my hands around them, open a window or door and gently set them free? Are ladybugs really that different from other bugs? Perhaps not to scientists, but they certainly make a better impression on me. I have a hard time stepping on a pretty little creature with red wings with black dots.

More and more research is proving "you never have a second chance for a first impression." First impressions made in a matter of seconds are rarely altered, even years later. Consequently, the first few seconds are absolutely "make it or break it" with everyone you meet, so it is essential that you give your appearance and the words you speak your utmost attention.

Do you exude a professional image that attracts others? Is

the first sentence that comes out of your mouth inviting and relatable? Is what you first say immediately perceived as relevant to the person you are talking to? Be at the top of your game every day in the way you look, what you say and...(read on!)

We often forgive those that bore us, but we
cannot forgive those that find us boring.
-Francois de la Rouchefoucauld, French classical author

IT'S NOT JUST WHAT YOU SAY...

...It's how you say it! What is it about charisma, enthusiasm and, most importantly, sincerity that sells? Why is it that two salespeople could have the same script and present the same information yet one will be far more successful than the other?

First impressions are a package deal. Your appearance and what you say are only a part of the package. The way in which you speak is a part as well (i.e., your inflection, your enthusiasm, your sincerity, etc.), and so is the way you listen. Actually, your nonverbal communication may make the biggest impression—-the firmness of your handshake, the warmth of your smile, whether your eye contact is direct or non-direct, whether your posture conveys that your are interested or apathetic, whether your listening is focused or not.

In fact, Dr. Albert Mehrabian, in his book *Silent Messages,* observed that the majority of interpersonal communication comes through non-verbal cues. He found that communication is...

> **55% visual (non-verbal communication such as eye contact, hand gestures and body language)**
>
> **38% voice quality (how you say what you say, including the volume, tone and inflection)**
>
> **7% words (what you actually say)**

If the above is true, the tone of what you say may be 5 times as important as what you say, and your body language and other methods of silent communication almost 8 times as important. The message here is that presentation skills are as important as the presentation itself, so devote time to working on them. Practice by yourself and practice with others. Videotape yourself giving a presentation. Then study the tape, listening to your words, observing your tone and watching your gestures. Would you buy from you?

Great expressions make great impressions.

ATTITUDE SELLS!

Over the years I have made calls with hundreds of account executives, each with his or her own level of experience, skill sets and talent. Some did exceptionally well over the course of their careers while others got frustrated and left the business after the excitement of their new position gave way to frustration with the difficulty of the process. In my opinion, the single biggest difference between success and failure in this business is "attitude." The cup of life is either "half full" or "half empty."

Everybody has a story. Few of us go through life unmarked by personal, professional or family events and circumstances that have had a profound effect on our lives. There is a direct correlation between how people approach life and whether or not they succeed. Those individuals who wake up every morning ready to seize the opportunities in life are the ones who "stumble" upon success.

The most successful people in this business share a common denominator …"a great attitude." It shines through in everything they do. A great attitude greatly improves the responsiveness and receptiveness of prospective clients, and it provides the additional energy needed to keep making those calls when everything isn't going as planned. It's important to realize that having a great attitude isn't a gift—-it's a personal choice that everyone can make every day. Choosing to be a positive influence will pay much greater dividends and will provide greater personal fulfillment.

I once had two new sales reps that began around the same time. They had comparable natural talents and comparable business experience. Both were exceptionally organized and excited about taking on the opportunities of their new position. However, after four weeks of making the calls while trying to orient themselves to the business, the difference between their attitudes became increasingly apparent. One channeled the frustration of not making more sales into a personal challenge to work harder and try to get as many new appointments as she could. The other rep seemed to focus her energy on her perceived failures and what was "not working." Her "half-empty cup" attitude immobilized the sales process, her initial confidence eventually giving way to a self-fulfilling prophecy of defeat.

Most experienced media sales reps, when asked, "What was your most exciting and most memorable year in the media business?" would say their first year. If asked, "What was your most challenging year in the media business?" most of them would again agree that it was year one. The first year is the "hump year" for most new media reps. One of every three new reps will probably not make it to year two. New reps should put on blinders in year one by diving into the trenches, learning everything they can and keeping a great attitude. After the first year, the skies seem to part with enlightenment, and as the learning curve begins to level out, both your effectiveness and productivity improve dramatically.

Your attitude is either the lock or the key
to the door of success.
-Source unknown

UNDERSTAND THE PERSONALITY
PROFILE OF YOUR CLIENTS

As a media sales rep, you will be exposed potentially to hundreds of different types of businesses, each with its own unique needs. In addition, you will deal with a number of different personality styles, each with a preferred way to communicate and a unique way of doing business. Understanding the motivations and touch points of your clients (and future clients) will help you determine what to present and the way to present it.

There have been many studies completed, many books written and a number of seminars presented on the topic of personality types. Every researcher and trainer has his or her own different classification of behavioral styles and how to work with them. While some classify by colors and others by names, there are similarities in the profiles. As far back as 400 BC Hippocrates identified the four temperament classifications: melancholic, phlegmatic, choleric and sanguine. Jung named them the feeler, thinker, sensor and intuitor. Coming from a little different perspective, the DISK profiles include the dominant, compliant, influencer and steadiness categories.

While few of us fit squarely in one categorical box, most of us have dominant traits that are easy to detect. The Merrill Reid classifications are defined as follows:

AMIABLE – Guided by feeling and intuition: appreciates relationships and the personal touch.

ANALYTICAL – Appreciates hard data, facts, research and any information to rationally justify a decision.

EXPRESSIVE – Usually outgoing and social, enjoys being of service, being useful and helping others.

DRIVER – Typically goal-oriented; likes being in control and will usually make quick decisions.

The more you can classify your prospects and your clients, the better you will be at presenting what they may want the way they want it. In addition, you will get a better idea of how to communicate with them on a day-to-day basis.

The first step is to understand your own personality profile.

We find it much easier to relate (and sell) to those who have personality profiles similar to our own. An amiable person, who cares much more about feelings and personal relationships, may have difficulty communicating with an analytical person, who places more importance on the facts and who makes decisions based on logic. Once you understand your client's (or prospect's) personality profile, you should tailor your approach and your presentation accordingly.

Different people have different motivations requiring different approaches.

UNDERSTAND THE PERSONAL NEEDS OF YOUR CLIENTS

Personal motivations absolutely play a part in most business decision making. You should take the time to ascertain why someone would decide to buy advertising from you. On one side of the spectrum is "pain" and on the other side is "opportunity."

PAIN	OPPORTUNITY
Defensive	**Offensive**
Fear as a motivator	**Opportunity as a motivator**
Losing customers, market share or money?	**More customers, market share and money!**
What's the cost of doing nothing?	**What's the lost revenue of not doing?**

The same client may be motivated by "opportunity" one day (or year) and "pain" the next. Much depends on their stage in the product life cycle, the competitive environment and current business climate. Pain can motivate change. If no changes are made to a marketing plan, it will be hard to expect different results. On the other side, a successful business flush in cash may easily invest additional funds for the opportunity to do even better.

Other clients may be the decision maker within a much larger organization. Appealing to how a marketing success could help their personal status within the organization may play into their decision-making process. Understand the personal motivations of your client (or prospect) and make sure that your presentation offers the right solutions.

> **People don't care what you know until**
> **they know that you care.**
> **-Source unknown**

ASK, LISTEN AND SPEAK

Many media sales reps stroll into a first meeting talking about "their" personalities and "their" rankings and "their" packages, before asking any questions about the prospective client's business. Oftentimes, they then spend more of their prospect's precious time negatively positioning other stations in the market. By the time they leave the appointment, they know little more about the person's business than when they came.

Most people have an impression of a superstar salesperson as being an "interesting extrovert." However, in this day and age, there may be an equal number of media sales superstars who are more the "interested introvert" type. It is more beneficial to spend your appointment time asking thoughtful questions about your clients and their businesses and then listening with interest to the answers they provide. Only then will you know more about where you can provide value when you speak.

If we were supposed to talk more than we listen, we would have two mouths and one ear.
-Mark Twain

UNDERSTAND THE BUYING INFLUENCES

We have been trained that you always meet with the decision maker, the one who writes the checks. Ultimately, that advice holds true. However, in many organizations you'll run into a maze of layers—gatekeepers and other barriers—keeping you from meeting with the one in charge. What do you do in these situations?

In 1985, Miller Heiman's landmark book *Strategic Selling* reinvented the selling process. It broke down the people who represent the buying influences that can impact your sale into the four types described below.

THE ECONOMIC BUYER – The ultimate decision maker who with one stroke can sign the approval or veto the deal.

THE TECHNICAL BUYER – A person who evaluates the specifications and screens out the bad deals. They can rarely approve the sale but can easily disqualify the offering. The advertising agency will usually be the technical buyer in media negotiations.

THE USER BUYER – The person who is involved in the day-to-day operations that may directly benefit from the increase in store traffic generated by the advertising (a store manager, a sales manager, etc.)

THE COACH – This is your inside champion, the person who will provide you information, guidance and direction on how best to proceed and who best to proceed with. (see next section)

In larger organizations, there are people that fit each of these roles. Each can play a positive role or a negative role in your selling process. More often than not, these people assume negative roles only when they have not been included in the process. Identify these player types with each of your prospects. Understand their roles and their personal motivations. If you can successfully show them how they can benefit through your plan, they will be instrumental in helping you make the sale.

> **He who has the gold makes the rule. He who works closely with the ruler has influence over the rules.**
> **-The "Golden Rule" of Sales**

HAVE A CHAMPION INSIDE THE BUSINESS

Everyone has always heard that "word-of-mouth" is the best source of advertising. Media advertising is word-of-mouth advertising on a broad scale. That same word-of-mouth exposure can be extremely beneficial *inside* an organization as well. There is nothing more beneficial than having an inside coach to explain the role everybody plays inside the company, to identify the buying influences and to help promote your involvement.

Since receptionists are usually the "gatekeepers" to the business owners, if you treat them well they can often be your "key" to the inside. Get to know them well. Ask them for their help in making an introduction. Explain how you can help their organization grow.

Although there may be only one final decision maker who can approve the sale, there can be many levels of people who have veto power before the decision reaches the top. By getting to know all the players and involving each one in the process, you will help minimize the possibility of being surprised in the 11th hour when the sale does not go through.

**Create word-of-mouth advertising
inside your prospect's doors.**

DEVELOP LONG-TERM RELATIONSHIPS

There are many advertising options, inside and outside of your medium, which could be effective in helping prospects grow their business, and every prospect has limited advertising funds available to spend. Much of the decision still comes down to "who they want to do business with" and "who they believe will do the best job for them." It may take you many meetings and many conversations before you get your first order, but effective communication, dedication and patience will pay off in the long run.

There will be times when you may be tempted to make short-term decisions that will not benefit the client (or you). The short-term billing gain could be a fraction of the long-term business loss that you will face if the program does not work. Stay the course and make good long-term business decisions.

We all experience days when we feel that we are "on top of the world." On those days that your attitude, perspective and zest for life (and your job) are overflowing, get out of the office as soon as possible and share your enthusiasm and positive energy with your clients and prospects. Don't waste these "good days" catching up on your paperwork. Hit the streets and begin building new long-term relationships.

**It takes twenty years to build a reputation
and five minutes to ruin it. If you think about that,
you will do things differently.
-Warren Buffett**

6. HOW TO WORK WITH ADVERTISING AGENCIES

THE AGENCY WORLD

Like all industries, the advertising agency world has been hit hard by consolidation, both with the companies they represent and with the agencies themselves. As a result, many agencies have responded by making severe cutbacks in staff. Following the lead of numerous companies in the corporate world, they are doing more with fewer people.

The opportunity for you is that agency buyers are always in need of good resources. They need people who they can rely on to give them objective, up-to-date information that can help them direct their buys. Each buyer may be handling a high volume of markets with each rep sending volumes of information. Simplicity is the key to standing out.

Most advertising agency campaigns involve more than one station and are usually directed by specific buying parameters. Advertising agencies place great importance on the efficiency of the schedule to achieve cost-per-point (CPP) or cost-per-thousand (CPM).

While most advertising agencies hopefully have the experience, confidence and marketing expertise to make an objective consideration of all opportunities in a given market, the "path of least resistance" for some is to go right to buying the top-rated shows or top-rated stations. This approach is the easiest to justify to the client and it takes no analysis other than a quantitative ranker. However, this approach is not fair to the media and it also does not benefit the client because:

- "Points don't buy products...people do." – Buying the top-rated shows/stations in the market does not guarantee the success of an advertising campaign.
- Rankers are based on ratings, which are based on one commercial – Advertisers do not buy "a commercial," they buy a campaign, which should be based on effective reach, frequency and efficiency.
- Other stations may fit the qualitative profile of the advertiser better, thereby producing a more efficient and more effective campaign.
- Other stations may be more cost effective by offering a lower cost-per-point (CPP) or cost-per-thousand (CPM), thereby saving advertising dollars or helping to extend an appropriated budget.
- Other stations may add on "real value" promotional sponsorships or campaigns (at no additional charge) that could help drive traffic.
- Buying just the top-rated stations or top-rated shows may be too costly on a limited budget to achieve the frequency and consistency necessary to be effective.
- Just because a total campaign is efficient (meets cost parameters) does not necessarily mean that it is effective (GETS RESULTS!)

**Show how you are right without making them wrong.
Position with finesse.**

PROVIDE VALUE TO ADVERTISING AGENCIES

While some of the smaller, one-man shops are open for creative suggestions, most of the larger agencies are looking for different qualities in a media rep, and most of these qualities center around "service." Though being a top-rated station will usually ensure being called on an avail, the agency world is a "relationship business." Most any station can be bought around if the media buyer does not believe they are being serviced well.

The time to position and sell the benefits of your station is *before* the buy comes down. Once the avail is sent over, it will be difficult to capture the attention that you and your station deserve. If a media buyer is buying six markets, and each market has ten stations, the buyer will be getting media kits and multiple calls from 60 different reps, usually with only a few days to place the buy.

If a media buyer were asked who the "best reps" in the marketplace were, a few names would probably be top of mind. Those are the reps who will be most successful in getting on the buy and garnering an "unfair share" of the agency's business for their station. The names of these top reps will be different, but the qualities that lead to their success will generally be the same. Here are some of the guidelines that top reps live by:

BE A RESOURCE – While most advertising agencies have access to the quantitative and qualitative numbers, most buyers do not have the time to keep up with the constant changes in the market. They usually have key reps that they trust to give them an "objective" analysis from their perspective.

BE HONEST - Not every station or program is the best choice for every buy. Buyers appreciate not being "sold" a suggested schedule that is not a good fit for the product or service being advertised. You will be better served in the long run by not trying to "sell" a fit that is not truly there.

BE RESPONSIVE – Get them *what* they want (not necessarily the rates), *when* they want it and *how* they want it. The agency business moves very quickly. It's not uncommon for a buy to come down with less than 24 hours turnaround. One of the biggest complaints that buyers have is the unresponsiveness of reps to calls and emails. Always try to return an agency phone call within 90 minutes. You will stand out!

BE THOROUGH – There are a lot of moving parts in media, with many opportunities for human error. If the contract is not checked for co-op or the wrong spot airs, the media buyer may question putting you on future buys. Always double check your work.

BE A PROBLEM SOLVER - When problems do arise (which they will), handle them quickly and efficiently, making sure the agency is satisfied with the solution. Communication is key.

BE A VALUE PROVIDER – You do not have to have the lowest rates or the lowest cost-per-point, but you do have to provide value for a buyer to put you on the buy. This value can come in many forms. It may be the exceptional service that you provide or an associated promotional campaign.

Different agencies and different buyers have different ideas on how they like to be serviced. It is best to understand the buyer's individual preferences by simply asking them: "How often would you like to be contacted?" and "What is the preferred method of communication...email or by phone?" Some overly aggressive sellers actually do more harm than good by making too many calls and taking too much time.

It is imperative to understand the expectations of the negotiation process with the buyer and with the agency. With agencies that go through many rounds of negotiation, it is best not to come in at your lowest rates first. On the other hand, with someone who needs a quick turnaround, you may want to come in with your best shot to ensure your position on the buy. If you come in expecting many rounds of negotiating and the buy has less than a 24-hour turnaround, you could get left at the gate with no call back and no money. Babs Scroggs, Media Director for Barber Martin in Richmond, Virginia, suggests it is best to ask the buyer to explain the buying process. Of course this will help you, but it will also make the buyer's job easier.

Make no mistake about it...if you take care of the buyer, the buyer has the power to take care of you! If you follow all of the advice above, making it easier for a buyer to do his or her job, you have a greater chance of getting an unfair share of the buy. That could mean getting placed on the buy even when you are not a top-rated station. It could mean getting a disproportionate share of the buy relative to your ratings. It could also mean getting incremental dollars in between the flights.

Commodities are interchangeable, individuals are not.

ADVERTISING AGENCY BUDGETS

Most major corporations have a fixed annual advertising budget. It is usually a top-down number that is established based on a fiscal revenue budget. From the VP of Marketing this number is typically transferred to the advertising agency Account Supervisor, Account Executive and Account Planner, who then help to determine the percentage breakdown for media placement. The budgets are then transferred to the Media Director who then relays the parameters of the buy (demo, gross rating points, cost-per-point, daypart distribution, etc.) through the Media Buyers to the various media partners. Media reps are left battling it out, positioning themselves to increase their "share" of the buy.

As a media rep, you are subject to a number of outside (uncontrollable) factors that will affect your billing. Media budgets can be reduced or even eliminated in a second. Wall Street demands growth in earnings, and if sales do not achieve a desired goal, advertising may be one of the first cuts (although it should be one of the last). Agencies are always in review. If they lose a key account, your billing could take a big hit. In addition, the fluctuation in your ratings can determine whether you get a buy, or at least can affect your rates and your total share. As a result, if you are heavily dependent on advertising agency revenue, your billing predictability will always be subject to factors beyond your control.

If your fortunes are tied to uncontrollable factors, your fortunes may be no more.

PROPOSING SCHEDULES TO ADVERTISING AGENCIES

The schedules that you present to advertising agencies may differ from the ones you typically present to direct accounts. Most agencies have a number of buying parameters that must be met to be included in the buy. They will most often use one of two cost efficiency buying parameters. Cost-per-point (CPP) is the cost of reaching an audience that is equivalent to one percent of the population in a given demographic in a stated universe. Cost-per-thousand (CPM) is the cost of delivering one thousand gross impressions with the proposed schedule.

Often, the CPP or CPM target may be much lower than prevailing station rates, which are priced primarily by supply and demand (with advertisers setting the rates). To be included on these buys, you will need to sell the value of your station and your services. You may also have to offer other promotional incentives to be considered. Some stations with high demand may come in above the cost-per-point. If not bought at the prevailing rates for this buy, the commercials will be sold to someone else. Other stations with lower demand (and lower inventory pressures) may come in below the cost-per-point, just to get on the buy.

Scheduling for agencies may take creativity, depending on what's acceptable to the client and what station management will approve. The following three possible scheduling techniques may be used to reduce the CPP or CPM without reducing the rates:

- Schedule more spots in the most efficient shows or most efficient dayparts.
- Narrow the timeframe or daypart to the more efficient hours.
- Include low-charge, broad rotators that fall in the best time available.

**The easier you make it for agencies to buy you,
the more they will buy you.**

7. HOW TO POSITION "THE NUMBERS"

RATINGS: WHAT DO THEY MEAN?

Ratings are simply a number (or percentage) that give the estimated number of people viewing or listening to station programs. Since they are based on a relatively small sample, they are subject to variations from ratings book to ratings book.

Radio terms and definitions can be obtained through Arbitron (www.arbitron.com) and television terms and definitions through Nielsen Media Research (nielsenmedia.com) or through the broadcast trade organizations (rab.com, tvorg and onetvworld.org). The problem is that even many experienced media reps do not truly understand ratings and how to explain their relevance to the advertiser. Learning as much as you can about Nielsen or Arbitron terms, definitions and applications will pay great dividends when you are sitting across the desk from a prospect or client and questions are asked.

Most of the confusion lies in learning just the technical definitions without understanding the relevance of the research. For example, in the radio world the technical definition of Average Quarter Hour Persons (AQH Persons) is "the average number of persons listening to a particular station for at least five minutes during a fifteen-minute period," whereas the more relevant description of AQH Persons to a client would simply be "the estimated number of people that will hear your commercial (within a specific demographic and specific time period)." The definition of "Cume Persons is "the total number of different persons who tune in to a radio station during the course of a daypart for at least five minutes," whereas to a client, cume simply represents the potential estimated audience that can be reached on a station (within a specific demographic and specific time period), similar to the circulation of a newspaper. The more commercials you air each week, the greater the percentage of the cume (weekly audience) that will be reached.

The better you understand ratings and their relevance from the advertiser's point of view, the more successful you will be at communicating their benefits. If you can get beyond the rankers and the "We're #1!" syndrome, there is extremely powerful information that can be used to help you and your clients plan their buy.

Understand meanings and applications, not just term and definitions.

LIVE BY THE SWORD—DIE BY THE SWORD

Ratings are a double-edged sword. While they represent one of the two primary measures of performance for management (ratings and sales), reliance on ratings is a dangerous place for salespeople to go. If your confidence in your station (and ultimately in yourself) is influenced by a half-a-point change in ratings, your success will be controlled by outside variables.

If the majority of your sales energy is spent boasting about your ratings increases relative to your competition in one ratings book, you are setting yourself up for the same argument to be used against you in the next ratings period. Ratings are not a "controllable factor" for salespeople, and because such a small sample size is used to establish ratings in most markets, they are subject to fluctuate. Good ratings can lull salespeople into believing that they are better than they are and can engender carelessness and complacency, while a sales rep at a lower-rated station has to develop a better skill set and understanding of their clients to sell beyond the numbers.

**Everyone's #1 somewhere sometime.
No one's #1 everywhere all the time.**

USE THE SWORD FOR ITS STRENGTHS

The purpose of ratings is to measure listenership or viewership in a given market. While station comparisons and book-to-book boasting (negative selling) will not be sustained in the long run, the estimates provided by the measurement sources can be powerful when used correctly. Individual ratings have little to do with the success of a campaign. Advertisers don't buy "a commercial," which is what most radio rankers are based on—they buy schedules and campaigns, which have little to do with "rankers."

A more meaningful measure for quantitative ratings is "cume" or "weekly viewship/listenership." This value reflects the weekly potential of prospects (potential reach). Whether your station's cume is 20,000; 200,000 or 2,000,000 the real question for your prospect is: "How many of these potential customers would it take to make a difference in your business?" Chances are, the answer is: "Very few."

Discuss the "real issues" of advertising in "real terms."

BRING YOUR PROFILE TO LIFE

What is the difference between 50,000 listeners/viewers and 100,000? How about 100,000 and 200,000? The average person can easily do the math but won't necessarily visualize the difference. To truly appreciate and communicate the power of your station, establish a familiarity with your local public event venues. For example, if your local arena seats 10,000 and your station's weekly audience (cume) is 100,000, ask your prospect to visualize the crowd at the last ballgame or concert he or she attended. A mental picture of a lot of people will emerge. Then explain that your station reaches the equivalent of *ten* sell-out-crowds on top of each other *each week*!

In the same way, you can paint a vivid picture of your station's profile. How do you usually describe the typical profile of your station or your station programs? A target of 25 to 54 is not a demographic...it is a family reunion. The listenership/viewership habits of a 25-year-old are dramatically different from those of a 54-year-old. While advertising agencies may list a "buying" demographic of 18 to 49 or 25 to 54, the core "programming" target age range for most radio stations and television programs will not exceed 20 years (with some exceptions).

For example, a Top 40 radio station may target teens through the mid-thirties and a smooth jazz station may target 35-to 54-year olds. By describing only the age cells of a listener/viewer, the profile is not "brought to life." For example if your target profile is a 25-to 44-year old with 2.5 children, add color to your presentation by describing your typical listener/viewer as a 35-year-old soccer mom or soccer dad. The mental picture will emerge of a well-dressed family stepping out of a nice minivan on a beautiful day, with fold-up chairs in tow on their way to the soccer fields.

People relate better to people rather than to numbers.

BRING YOUR QUALITATIVE PROFILE TO LIFE

When advertising agencies refer to "ratings" and "rankers," they are referring to a quantitative methodology based on one commercial. Furthermore, quantitative ratings assume that "all people are created equal." A point (Gross Rating Point or GRP) is just a point. The reality is that "points do not buy products—people do."

All stations and station programs are not created equal. Each one has its unique characteristics that attract a different audience. While you are *buying* a series of programs, what you are *receiving* is delivery of a specific audience. It's not that one type of audience is better than another; it's just that one type of audience will fit the target profile of your prospect better than another.

While many people can understand high indexing categories, most prospects will relate better to real people as opposed to percentages. For example, if your qualitative research shows that an estimated 16,000 of your station's listeners plan on buying new furniture in the next 12 months (128 index) at an average expenditure of $500, your listeners would represent $8,000,000 in buying power to the furniture store being presented. You should emphasize to the prospect that "they're going to buy their furniture somewhere—why not have them consider your store?"

While all your numbers may be impressive to you, all the client cares about is "What do they all mean to me?"

THE QUALITATIVE SELL – BE CAREFUL

All stations are quick to portray their elite viewership or listenership with high disposable income, and they all have the qualitative research to back up their claims. As with most statistical research, there are more than enough qualitative categories that any station in the market can massage the numbers and bend the output to prove its point. These high-end qualitative profiles may benefit you when it comes to selling expensive automotives or investment services, but the reality is that most companies that advertise on your station are not targeting the elite. The majority of advertisers appeal to the "masses," not the "classes."

By profiling your station *before* you uncover the target demographic of your prospect, you risk pigeonholing yourself into a defined market that will not benefit you or your prospect. An example is a swimming lake that I had prospected while working as an account executive at a Top 40 radio station. When I first met with the owner to present our marketing services, he asked me to describe the economic profile of our listeners. I told him that "our profile reflects that of a theme park. The appeal of great new music has no economic boundaries—our listeners live in trailer parks and in 4,000-square-foot homes."

He seemed to appreciate the answer in light of a recent appointment he had with a rep from a country music station in the market. He told me that when he had asked the other rep the same initial question, he was presented with piece after piece profiling the upscale listenership of country music. While the stereotypical country music fan was blue-collar with little disposable income, the station's "new research" showed that its typical listeners were executives with six-figure incomes and expensive cars who liked to take exotic trips. After the meeting he had thanked the rep for her time but explained that his lake's clientele were lower to middle income at best. He stated further that if the station's country music listeners could afford all those expensive things, he was sure they would just as soon spend the extra money necessary to vacation at the beach instead of swimming in his dirty little lake.

The next day the country music rep returned to explain that the "real" country music research showed that their primary market was a lower-income clientele that exactly matched his target profile. The owner asked the rep to leave and never to return. While the country music station's listenership probably fit the "real" profile of the lake's patrons, the account rep's reputation was forever ruined.

Always uncover the profile of your prospects' customers before positioning the profile of your listeners and viewers.

FEATURES TELL, BUT BENEFITS SELL

The features/benefits positioning is one of the oldest, but still one of the most effective, positioning strategies in sales. In the media world, we have feature sheet after feature sheet that promote our station, our programs, our personalities and corresponding facts, figures and data supporting our claims that we are number one (somewhere). Our prospects and our clients patiently follow along, but inside they are saying "Why should I care?"

While we present our information with evident pride and self interest, as if we were showing off pictures of our newborn baby, our clients have heard it all hundreds of times before and really do not care. Therefore, when information is being presented, it is imperative that the benefits to the client are clearly communicated.

If you have research that shows that you have 20,000 listeners who plan to buy a new car at some point during the next twelve months at an index of 145 (feature), you should explain how this fact "benefits" the client. Communicate to the client that a commercial campaign on your station has the potential to reach 20,000 "now buyers," and your station is 45% more efficient than other stations in the market for new car buyers. The bottom line is that you believe you can give the client a greater return on their investment than an equivalent buy on other stations.

Marketing is not a battle of products;
it's a battle of perceptions.
-Noel Peebles, author

8. HOW TO MAKE THE MOST OF YOUR TIME

ALL WE HAVE IS TIME

All we have is time – period! *It is our most important asset* – period! It is the money-producing asset of your organization (i.e., commercials) and, more importantly, it is ALL WE HAVE personally. There are 24 hours in each day——that's 1,440 minutes or 86,400 seconds. Lost hours in the day are lost opportunities, and lost opportunities represent revenue lost.

Most people in the media world believe their major competition is other media or other members of the same media. So much time is spent trying to position and re-position "the other guys" instead of getting the most out of what we can offer (individually, as a company and as a medium).

Most successful media reps understand that their biggest competition comes not from "the other guys," but rather from "the clock." Every day is a race against time. When you wake up in the morning, it's like turning over an hourglass and the hourglass will be empty at the end of the day.

Remember, being "busy" does not mean you are being "effective." A hamster on a wheel is busy, but he does not make it too far. Make sure that you distinguish between the "urgent," the "important," and the "insignificant distractions." Wherever you put your time, focus and energy is where you will get your results.

Most star salespeople in the business have a system to get the most out of every day. One of the most critical components to success in this industry is determining the best use of your time on a daily and hourly basis. Those who excel can distinguish between the "urgent" and the "important." How do you plan your day? How do you prioritize your next activity? How do you decide what prospect or client to call? Increase your effort, improve your efficiency and greater results will follow.

Effort + Efficiency = RESULTS

BE "THE ORGANIZED EXECUTIVE"

In her book, *The Organized Executive*, Stephanie Winston draws a correlation between organization and productivity and shares many strategies for improvement. Have you ever had days when you have a "hard time getting off the ground?" Days where you find yourself pushing paper, but the paper doesn't go away? Paper can prevent productivity during the day. Organization is a challenge for many salespeople. Most would rather be out doing, rather than in organizing. However, the challenge is that unless you spend the time to plan out *what* you are doing and *where* you are going, you may be going—but going in the wrong direction.

I recommend two forms of organizing. One is "front end organizing," which deals more with the strategic and planning side (who to call, what to do, when to do, where to go, etc.). This process keeps you more focused, more efficient and ultimately more productive. Days begun with a direction and a purpose are more likely to lead to greater results. Therefore, spend fifteen minutes to a half-hour each morning setting your priorities for the day. What projects do you need to complete? What people do you need to meet? What proposals do you need to write so you can feel like a success at the end of the day?

The second form of organizing is "back-end organizing," which involves taking care of the business that you have created (organizing, setting up files, filing, etc.). The more disorganized that you are in this area, the more overwhelmed you will be. Finish each day by "back-end organizing" your day for fifteen minutes to a half-hour. When you start off each day fresh, you will naturally become more productive.

While light organizing is needed on a continual basis, at least twice a year a total "catharsis," or total cleansing and organizing of files is needed. Just before the 4th of July and just before the end of the year, go through every file to discard any papers no longer needed that are just taking up space. If you believe you will need to review information at a future point in time, clip the papers together in your files or box them away (so you will not have to review again). I've found that I can reduce the size of myfiles to half their original size or less!. Drawers that you have had a hard time opening and shutting will once again glide effortlessly back and forth. It will give you tremendous peace of mind!

Efforts and courage are not enough
without purpose and direction.
-John F. Kennedy

COMPARTMENTALIZE YOUR PRIORTITIES

Few positions in the business world have as much freedom, yet also as much responsibility, as the position of media sales. It requires the determination and self discipline to make sales calls, the creative marketing savvy to develop promotional ideas and the detail orientation to keep all the traffic orders, production deadlines and promotional commitments in place. Even with a well-thought-out plan, your daily schedule can seem overwhelming and at times confusing when it comes to prioritizing what to do next.

As an account executive, you may feel overwhelmed with your daily "to do list" and have difficulty concentrating on the job at hand. For example, while trying to write copy you could lose focus by allowing other upcoming tasks for the day to bleed into your concentration. The result would be bland copy and a lack of satisfaction from doing anything well, because part of your attention would be focused on all the remaining tasks at hand. Give full attention to only one thing at a time.

Only when you start "compartmentalizing" your focus will you be able to realize your full potential. By "compartmentalizing," I mean determining the priorities of the day and then channeling your total concentration, focus and energy into the single task of the moment without allowing the remaining responsibilities of the day to bleed into your consciousness. The result will not only be better work, but also a more calming sense of purpose and completion as one project after another is successfully checked off your "to do list." You may not get through everything on your list, but you will have piece of mind knowing that the most "important" projects are complete.

In fact, "compartmentalization" can play a critical role in improving one's quality of life. The ability to block out future tasks, responsibilities and projects on your personal "to do list" as well as variables outside of your immediate control and to instead focus on taking care of the immediate task at hand can greatly reduce your overall stress level. In his book *Don't Sweat the Small Stuff...And It's All Small Stuff,* author Richard Carlson suggests that your "in box" will always be full. He says that "the purpose in life is not to get it all done, but to enjoy each step along the way."

How do you eat an elephant? One bite at a time.
-Source unknown

9. HOW TO STAND OUT FROM THE CROWD

WHY CLIENTS BUY YOU

Roy Williams, an outstanding "ad" man, speaker, trainer and author, defines sales as "the transfer of confidence." Why do your clients buy (or consider buying) from you? I contend that there are four factors:

They like you and trust **you.**
They like your **station/programs.**
They trust your **expertise.**
They are sold on your **results.**

The old saying "it's not what you know…it's who you know" could be changed to "it's what you know AND who you know." Knowing people will help you get in the door, and may help you make the first sale. Ultimately, however, it will be what you know—-your expertise and the results that you can deliver—-that will determine your long-term success. Regardless of how much your clients "like you" or are fans of your station and its programs, it is your ability to provide a "Return on Investment" that will keep them buying your services.

**The secret to success is to know something
that nobody else knows.
-Aristotle**

WHAT'S YOUR UNIQUE PERSONAL VALUE (UPV)?

We all have reputations, whether we like it or not. The good news is that you create your reputation each day, with every conversation you engage in and with every action you take (or choose not to take). What *are* you known for? What do you *want* to be known for? If others would describe you the way you would like to be described, then the two are in alignment. If not, there might be a gap between others' perceptions of you and reality (in which case, some serious PR is needed) or you might have a distorted view of reality (in which case you need to look at the way you do things and make some modifications).

Few companies in reality have a truly "unique" selling proposition that no one else has. If one does, it won't be long before others copy the successful concept (and possibly make it better). But, every individual truly is unique and close personal relationships can't be replicated. Everyone has what I call a Unique Personal Value (UPV). Your UPV has nothing to do with the station you sell. It has little to do with how well you schedule commercials or give added value. Rather, it is what you do for your clients that truly sets you apart. Is it your endearing personality, your business savvy, your outside-the-box ideas or your world-class service? If you were not a part of the equation, what would be missed? That's your UPV!

If the ten top advertising clients in your market were asked

"Who are the best reps in the market?" what names would come to mind first? Why? What is it that makes them "the best?" What qualities and characteristics do they have, and what is it that they do day after day to become "top of mind" with their clients? My guess is that they do not stand out by offering the lowest rates. These individuals are perceived to be "top-notch" because each of them offers some "Unique Personal Value" that other individuals in the market do not.

Develop your UPV. Live your UPV. Promote your UPV. Until you do, your perceived value will be directly anchored to your station and its ratings and rates. In this scenario, you are an expendable commodity, with your place in the equation easily filled by another rep at another station with higher ratings offering a better deal. If, on the other hand, you work to develop your UPV, your perceived value will be determined by the solutions that you present and the results that you deliver—-things for which *you* can take charge.

As Jim Collins states in the opening paragraph of *Good to Great*, "Good is the enemy of great." Don't settle for a reputation of "goodness" or you will never achieve "greatness." While you may "work" for another company, in many ways you operate more like an independent contractor having your own business. It is *you* that they are buying, as much as your station, and it is *your* reputation as a trusted advisor that will precede you wherever you go.

When a good reputation precedes, success follows!

PROVIDE WORLD-CLASS SERVICE

What is "world-class service?" It is the talk of many in service industries but the reality of few. World-class service will greatly exceed service expectations on a consistent basis. When a client is provided with world-class service, it often becomes a legendary experience that is retold to others in a form of free publicity that cannot be bought. In the international arena, Nordstrom is one of the first names that comes to mind. In the book *The Nordstrom Way*, Robert Spector profiles how Nordstrom reinvented the retail customer service experience. One of Nordstrom's most legendary stories was about a refund given for tires bought at a closed store where a Nordstrom had since been built. They did not want to have a dissatisfied customer, regardless of the fact that the tires were not even bought there. Megan Becker, General Manager of the Richmond, Virginia, Nordstrom, keeps the customer service dream alive by hanging a tire in the employee hallway. On the tire is written, "Create your own tire story," an inspiring reminder to do whatever it takes to keep a customer satisfied.

World-class service is not limited to national or international companies. The following are two examples of world-class service that I have experienced at the local level. While on vacation at the Homestead Resort, a five-star resort in western Virginia, I realized that I had forgotten to bring cuff links, part of my planned outfit for eating in the formal dining room. Fortunately, they had a fine men's shop on the premises. The problem was that I did not need (or want) to buy expensive new cuff links for just one night. When I explained my dilemma to the manager of the shop, he said, "Not a problem," and encouraged me to pick out any pair in the store to borrow for the night, asking only that I return them in the morning. I tried to give him proof of identification, my room key and a credit card for collateral, but he said that there was no need for that and to just enjoy the evening. That's world-class service!

Another world-class service experience of mine occurred at the locally owned Midas of Richmond in Virginia. A while back, after being in the shop for some costly repairs, my wife's car broke down again shortly thereafter. We called Mark Smith, the owner of the shop where we had taken the car, and he personally came out to our house to try to jump the car. When this failed, he called his towing service to pick up the car and drove my wife to rent a minivan at his expense. He had the primary wiring harness on our car rebuilt, also at his expense. He spent over $1,200 out-of-pocket, but he would not accept payment because he said the problem was something that he should have caught the first time. Midas of Richmond now has a customer for life that is worth many times more than the $1,200, not to mention all the referral business they receive from my repeated telling of the story.

While both of these examples exemplify world-class service, the Midas episode shows that "you never lose business over a problem...only the way it is handled." If a problem is handled quickly and communicated effectively, your reputation may even be enhanced (see later chapter).

What can you do to provide world-class service in your media sales world? If your clients were asked which of their media reps provides the best service in the market, would they name you? Each of your clients is different, with different needs and different desires. While concert tickets and theme park passes may be appreciated, they are not unique—other stations have the same perks. What they don't have is *you.*

Provide a reason for your clients to tell their story about you and the unique advantage you give them. Hold yourself accountable to the highest standards of customer service every day. Exceed expectations and your clients will help you exceed budgets!

Strive for world-class service on a local level every day.

ADD "REAL VALUE" AS OPPOSED TO "ADDED VALUE"

In the world of media sales, the term "added value" has come to refer to a quick and dirty appeasement of an advertising agency's request for an avail. It may be news/traffic/weather sponsorships, a promotional tie-in or a free remote that may do little to help the client's business and may actually hurt your station's reputation if no one shows up. In other words, what typically passes for an "added value" might, in reality, have a neutral or negative effect—-the opposite of what is intended.

Instead of just providing cookie-cutter "added value," you must strive to provide "real value" by uncovering what it is that will truly benefit a client. As an example, Victory Lady Fitness, a women's workout facility, had two ways to increase membership. One was to motivate more women who did not know about the club to visit the club and consider joining. The second was to motivate the membership salespeople to give tours of the club and sign up as many new members as possible. The conversion of prospects to members was critical to the club's success.

Our station came up with a package plan to help out on both fronts. A concentrated afternoon drive commercial schedule helped accomplish the first goal. To help motivate/reward the club's membership salespeople, we initiated a monthly sales award for the top membership seller. The award was a nice dinner for two and other station spiffs, which we were able to provide through in-house trade. Out of all the information and possibilities we presented, it was this incentive award that excited the owner the most.

If it is not *real* value, it doesn't *add* value.

RETAIN OLD-FASHIONED VALUES

In this age of corporate scandals and self-serving greed, there is a general mistrust of being "sold a bill of goods," especially with such an intangible product as broadcast advertising. Now more than ever before, the integrity factor will play a larger role in people's decision making about whom to trust with their hard earned funds. Few business owners truly understand how to make broadcast advertising work, so they are relying solely on the ability and credibility of the media rep.

While it takes time to earn someone's deep trust, most people want to see the good in other people and will form a trusting or distrusting impression of a salesperson almost immediately. After making a trusting first impression with a client, it is up to you *never* to let that person down. Stephen

R. Covey in his book *The 7 Habits of Highly Effective People* refers to what he calls the "emotional bank account." It is a metaphor that describes the amount of trust that has been built up in a relationship. "Deposits" of trust are built up over time through courtesy, kindness and honesty. If an event happens that "withdraws" trust, there is hopefully a large enough "reserve" built up to prevent the relationship from being severed.

In the business world, the same theory could hold true for a "confidence bank account." A quick sale may be made to a client one time, but that person's confidence in you may be broken forever if that sale doesn't achieve the desired results. *Always* do what's in the best interest of your clients. This will build their faith in your ability and credibility and keep your "confidence bank account" healthy.

In the last analysis, what we are communicates far more effectively than anything we say or do. -Stephen R. Covey, author, speaker and consultant

MAKE PRESENTATIONS TO IMPRESS!

In this day of multimedia, many radio and television stations still rely on one-dimensional one-sheets as their primary source for station presentations. We have all seen our client's expressions as we roll out page after page of one-sheets promoting our products, our promotions, our positioning and our personalities. Let's face it: we are all #1 somewhere, and our clients have heard and seen it all.

We are in a technologically-driven entertainment business, and while we do need to present some information about our stations, the most effective way to capture the essence of what we do is through the use of multimedia. A five- to ten-minute station presentation developed in a program such as Flash or PowerPoint can be created with pictures, music and video clips that can bring your station's programs, promotions and personalities to life. Testimonials can be positioned using a series of edited video clips or audio clips of clients expressing their positive experiences with your station.

We are in the media business! We are in the business to entertain and to inform. Our stations spend thousands of dollars on promotions to make favorable impressions with viewers and listeners, in an attempt to win ratings. We need to spend a little extra time and money creating presentations to impress our advertisers as well. After creatively telling your "short" story, the majority of the meeting should be centered on hearing the client's story.

Station presentations should be "show and tell to sell!"

SWEAT THE SMALL STUFF

While it is not emotionally healthy to sweat all the small stuff in life, in many respects the reverse is true when it comes to managing priorities in the media world. Few sales industries have as many "moving parts" or factors with so many processes being influenced by so many people, any one of which has the potential to influence the final outcome in a negative way. Is the order filled out correctly (i.e., dates, time periods rates, coop, etc.)? Have you truly represented the goal of the campaign to your copywriter through your copy points? Will the commercial be produced with enough time to play it to the client and make any changes desired? The list goes on and on. The more organized you are and the more attention you pay to every contributing factor, the better you will be able to manage the entire process and direct a favorable outcome.

While the Disney Corporation is widely known for unequalled creativity, they have always said that "the magic is in the details." Check and double-check your details. The goal is to catch any problem before it reaches the viewer, listener or the advertiser. Sweat the small stuff, so that your clients don't have to.

An ounce of prevention is worth a pound of cure.
-Benjamin Franklin

YOU NEVER LOSE BUSINESS OVER A PROBLEM – ONLY THE WAY IT IS HANDLED.

Even with your best efforts to prevent them, there will be times when problems arise. This is when you need humility, rational judgment, timely communication and effective solutions to correct the problem and get things back on a positive footing.

Mike Cutchall, a broadcast executive and one of my mentors, has always said, "Most problems are 80% systems and 20% people, yet we tend to focus 80% of our blame on the people." If it has not already happened, at some point you will be faced with a situation where your station missed spots or ran the wrong spots. It is best to take the high road quickly to inform a client of a mistake (before they find out on their own), accept responsibility on behalf of the station (without placing blame) and ask what can be done to make up for it. When possible, give back more than they would expect in return.

Our station once had a client who was sold a booth sponsorship to a huge street festival. Somehow in the logistics phase of the project, his company's name was omitted from the festival line-up. Unfortunately, when the supplemental staff he had hired for the day showed up ready to work, there was no table, tent, chairs or exhibit space reserved for them. With nowhere to set up, the staff just left and went home.

As the station's General Manager, I received a distressing call from the client on Monday morning. He was furious over the problem, especially about how bad it made him look inside the company. I apologized profusely and accepted personal responsibility for the problem (although I had no direct personal responsibility, the problem occurred on my watch). I followed up with an apologetic letter offering him a free make-good campaign at his convenience. I also wrote a second letter for him to post at his office taking full responsibility for the problem and apologizing to his staff for any inconvenience. He called me as soon as he received the letters to thank me for my actions and quick response; and he affirmed that he looked forward to continuing our relationship in the future.

To reinforce the chapter heading, "you never lose business over a problem—-only the way it is handled." If you handle a problem quickly, decisively and communicate to your client what action was taken, your personal reputation (and your station's reputation) may even be enhanced.

When you confront a problem, you begin to solve it.
-Rudolph Giuliani, former Mayor of New York City

USE THE "MAGIC WORDS" OFTEN

We learned them early on as children, but their usefulness and effect are timeless—the words "thank you" still ring sweet as a show of personal appreciation. Whether you are thanking people for their time, their consideration or their business, the words cannot be said too many times. It just feels good to be a recipient of a "thank you." Since with these two words it really is true "the more, the better," write it as well as saying it. Sending "thank you" notes for a prospect's time not only shows your appreciation but also reinforces your name to a deciding prospect.

People appreciate being appreciated. Unfortunately, in today's fast-paced, get-it-done-yesterday, meeting-a-minute world, the "thank you's" do not come often enough. Taking the "little" extra time to say a sincere "thank you" will produce magical results over and over again!

Your greatest return on investment will come from invest-
ing your breath in the two words "thank you!"

THE
BUSINESS
OF
ADVERTISING

10. HOW TO THINK LIKE A MARKETER

TIME TO CHANGE HATS

OK, now you are in the door. You have sold yourself an audience for your presentation. You have obviously made a compelling case that you can help the prospect with the only thing *they* really care about—increasing *their* sales. Now it's time to take off your "sales" hat, put on your "marketing" hat and take care of business—*their* business!

As stated earlier, your clients don't really care about your station, your shows, your personalities or anything about your business as much as they care about their own businesses. Therefore, 80% of the time you spend with your prospects and clients should be spent talking about *their* challenges and *their* opportunities. Especially during your first appointment with a prospect, most communication should be in the form of *asking* and *listening*—not *telling*.

Effective marketing is part art and part science, part common sense and part uncommon creativity. The "problem" is that creating effective marketing campaigns is extremely difficult and can take a lot of time. The "opportunity" is that most people in this profession do not spend the necessary time and energy to be truly successful in the "business of advertising."

Most media reps inadvertently go by an 80/20 rule when

it comes to the sales of advertising versus the business of advertising. The average media rep will spend 80% of his or her time prospecting, setting appointments, and preparing for appointments to "sell advertising." That leaves only 20% of one's time to spend on client uncoveries, market research, formulating strategic marketing plans and developing creative campaigns that are designed to get results.

The problem is that for most sales reps, their training has been centered on developing "their" sales techniques (i.e., prospecting, presenting, closing, etc.). Most of their communication with sales management is centered on "their" sales process (i.e., number of appointments, dollars asked for business, station billing, etc.) and most of their recognition is centered on "their" sales results (i.e., percentage of budget, new business goals, etc.).

It's not that the above elements are unimportant or that the "sales of advertising" techniques should be ignored; the station's profitability and media rep's income obviously depend on station sales. If an equal amount of time were spent on the "business of advertising," then the client's campaigns would be more effective, the client's business would grow and the end result would be a satisfied customer. This satisfied client would then be more likely to continue to advertise, thus resulting in greater sales and less attrition. Also, satisfied clients spread the word to others, creating additional, "free" referral business. The bottom-line effect is that budgets would be achieved, management conversations would be more positive, and rewards and recognition would follow.

The purpose of a business is to satisfy their customers, not to make money. Making money is the offshoot.
-Peter Drucker, writer, teacher and consultant

IT'S A JUNGLE OUT THERE

Today's business environment has become increasingly complex and competitive due to the dramatic changes brought on by globalization. In today's marketplace there is increasing product proliferation, brand erosion, market segmentation, consumer skepticism and time poverty, rendering traditional marketing plans obsolete. Life cycles are now three years or less, whereas they used to be seven years or more. The exponential increase in the speed at which technology has progressed has resulted in new products coming to market faster, at reduced costs, and, often, before a market demand has been established.

Almost every product category has reached a stage of technological development at which the *capacity* to produce dwarfs the consumer's *demand* to purchase. As a result, manufacturing facilities are being shut down, offshore contracts are increasing to reduce the production costs and additional incentives and rebates are being offered just to keep products moving (to reduce the inventory costs).

We are now living in a world of "TMI"—too much information. Everywhere we turn there is another billboard, street sign, bus sign or advertisement vying for our attention and ultimately our pocketbook. While some experts estimate the range of impressions to be up to 3,000 per day, Media Dynamics estimates in TV Dimensions 2005 that "the typical adult has the opportunity to view, read or hear (via TV, radio, magazines, newspapers and the internet) 294 ads daily; however, of these, only 53% or 157 ads gain any degree of scanning or attention. In all probability, only 10-20 of these ads have a real impact on the viewer, listener or reader, sufficient to stimulate some interest in the brand." We filter or tune out most ads for survival.

For example, if you are buying a new car there is an *overwhelming* number of makes and models, not to mention a high number of dealerships to choose from. Formerly "value provider" automotive manufacturers are creeping up in the higher price ranges, and companies like Mercedes Benz are now offering cars in the lower price ranges, trying to capture a younger market and build a customer for life. Consumers are extremely confused when it comes to what to buy and where to buy, and dealerships are challenged on how to reach this moving target.

What implications does this situation present for you at your local retail level? Your clients and prospects in every industry are on the front lines fighting for survival every day. They need someone to see the forest through the trees and help them determine a direction.

> **"Hell, there are no rules here — we are just trying to accomplish something."**
> **-Thomas Edison**

BE A JUNGLE GUIDE

Complex problems call for complex solutions. It will take more than good relationships, trust and empathy to deal with today's marketing challenges. While these value-related qualities are critical for success, they are not sufficient alone. To be truly, maximally successful, you will need a real understanding of the problems your clients are facing. As part analyst, part consultant and part business advisor your success will depend on your expertise in making recommendations, providing solutions and seizing opportunities to help grow your clients' businesses.

It is very difficult to put yourself in the mindset of a customer. It is much easier to try to sell a weekend blitz. You must understand that your prospects and clients are working harder than ever trying to thrive and survive with increasingly lower margins. They are more focused on "product and process," their areas of expertise. They often do not have the time to look forward. Where they need your help is on "marketing and promotion," or how to increase their customer base and move more of their product or service (your area of expertise).

The businesses that survive in tomorrow's marketplace will be the ones that are able to adapt to change and anticipate future needs. They will have to be better, faster, more efficient and more creative to compete. Your marketing expertise can help provide another perspective. Explain to your clients *why* they need to promote and *how* to promote their goods and services.

It is not the strongest of the species that survive, nor the most intelligent, but the ones most responsive to change.
-Charles Darwin

MARKETING: AN EXPENSE OR AN INVESTMENT?

Every operating business has its share of fixed operating costs (personnel wages, rent, utilities, insurance, etc.)—expenses that do not fluctuate with sales levels. Each also incurs variable operating costs (cost of goods sold, commissions, etc.) that increase or decrease accordingly in direct relation to sales volume.

Most companies are limited by their line-item expense category called "advertising." It is often set as a percentage of sales and is often based on historical numbers. The problem with this formula is that it can lead to a self-fulfilling deteriorating spiral. Acting on this theory, an automotive dealer whose sales start declining may slash the dealership advertising budget. As a result, future sales numbers drop further, as the message continually gets diluted, and the downward spiral in sales will continue with each successive advertising budget cut.

Adopting a more growth-oriented philosophy, companies should instead consider allocating a percentage of their anticipated (future) sales to marketing and advertising. Japanese business leaders have traditionally viewed marketing and advertising as an investment rather than an expense. Unfortunately for American companies, Wall Street expectations and short-term profit goals often drive short-term (and short-sighted) decision making, which can lead to the decreasing marketing budgets.

Local companies need to understand the need to invest in their future by marketing. Oftentimes, start-up businesses invest thousands of dollars on their location, their inventory and their operating expenses, leaving few dollars to promote the fact that they are even open for business.

Bo Randall, an agency friend of mine used an analogy to explain the benefits of advertising to his client, a large automotive group. He drew a parallel between advertising and putting your foot on the gas pedal when driving. It takes a lot of gas to get the car moving forward but less gas to keep the momentum once it is established. If you take your foot off the gas, the car will continue to move forward but the momentum will decrease until the car eventually comes to a stop. Most business owners will understand this analogy. The first goal however is to convince them of the need to get in the car and put their foot on the gas.

If you do not advertise, there is a good chance that no one will see you, hear you or even know about you (regardless of how good your products or services are).
-Source unknown

THE GOALS OF MEDIA ADVERTISING

Why do businesses advertise? While there would be many stated reasons from your advertisers, the majority of the answers would revolve around their desire to increase sales. While the ultimate goal of advertising would be to increase sales, a host of other mindsets must be influenced (buying cycles) before a motivation to purchase will be triggered. Just as a prospective client does not care about your station's advertising sales goals, most consumers are not concerned about helping to make a retailer's season. All they care about is "what's in it for them." An advertising campaign should always answer that question.

Some of the best marketing books, which address the question "Why do people do the things they do?" were written by Roy Williams. His books *The Wizard of Ads*, *Secret Formulas of the Wizard of Ads*, and *Magical Worlds of the Wizard of Ads*, address the psychology of advertising and how the brain functions to relate to the decision making process of consumers. He asserts that you have to reach people's hearts before you can reach their pocketbooks. Why does Jerry Lewis bring the children on stage at his annual MDA Labor Day Telethon? He knows that the more people are able to identify with the *kids*, the more likely they are to make a donation to the *cause*.

Michael Corbett, in his book *33 Ruthless Rules of Advertising* suggests that the purpose of advertising is "to create an equity position in a target market and to reach and motivate a sufficient number of consumers so that a business can reach a specific growth objective." He defines an "equity position" as when people think of your business when they have a need for the products or services that you sell. This goal is not achieved over a weekend blitz or even over a short schedule. It takes time, energy and commitment from the advertiser and the media rep to make advertising successful.

I believe that the purpose of media advertising is to achieve three sequential goals to be effective. These goals are to generate consumers':

Share of Mind (and heart) - commonly called "Top of Mind Awareness," which is created by "branding" a company and forming an emotional bond between the consumers and the company's product(s) or services.

Share of Time – motivating consumers to take action by calling or visiting the company (physically or via website).

Share of Dime (it rhymes better than "dollar") – the final step, which involves being convinced that the value of a product or service is worth making a purchase.

Advertising may be used to *fill* a demand (need, want or desire) or to *create* a demand (need, want or desire). But it should always be an important component of an overall marketing plan for growing businesses. Expectations of a campaign should be clearly defined by the client. These expectations should be realistic in the mind of the media rep. Also, these expectations should be measurable, so it is possible to determine the effectiveness of the advertising.

Regardless of the goal of a campaign—-to enhance an image, to educate consumers, to introduce a new product or products, to promote a sale or to position the company—it is only rarely that clients see quick results through broadcast advertising. New advertisers often expect the phone to start ringing immediately and traffic to begin swarming as soon as the commercials hit the air. Therefore, it is always a good idea to diffuse these expectations by underpromising and hopefully overdelivering on results.

We want to sell air, and they want to buy results. The more results we sell, the more air they buy.

CROSS OVER THE TIPPING POINT

In the book *The Tipping Point*, Malcolm Gladwell suggests that the emergence of fashion trends or the transformation of unknown books to bestsellers is like an epidemic. "Ideas and products and messages and behaviors spread just like viruses do," until they reach the tipping point. It all starts with one person telling others, who tell others, creating what we commonly call "word-of-mouth advertising" that pushes a company, product or service into high demand.

Gladwell defines three characteristics that lead to the tipping point:
- Contagiousness
- Little causes can have big effects
- Change happens not gradually, but at one dramatic moment.

Media advertising, if implemented successfully can perpetuate the tipping point, by moving mass numbers of people to change their beliefs and behaviors, and spreading the word to others, who spread the word to others. The goal is to help your clients be known in their target market as "the hot restaurant" or "the trendiest place to shop."

A brand for a company is like a reputation for a person. You earn reputation by trying to do hard things well. -Jeff Bezos, founder and CEO of Amazon.com

11. HOW TO GATHER INFORMATION ON YOUR CLIENT

THE CUSTOMER NEEDS ANALYSIS

Too often the media have been guilty of presenting advertising packages, schedules and promotions before ever meeting with a prospect to uncover their individual needs, opportunities and goals. Prescribing an advertising plan without diagnosing the prospect's business is like a doctor prescribing a treatment plan before ever knowing where the patient hurts.

All sales trainers, sales managers and even many media companies have their own definitions of what is called a Customer Needs Analysis (CNA). The names and the format may differ. Some prefer a standard form with standard questions, whereas others prefer a series of questions customized to the client and the specific industry. Still others like to use a flowing, unscripted series of open-ended questions that may lead to hidden nuggets of need. Regardless of the form it takes, there is nothing more important in marketing than the "uncovery" process.

It is imperative to meet with the decision maker (i.e., the one who writes the check or the one who can approve the check) when it comes to presenting the advertising plan for approval. However, the CNA process may be started before your first appointment. For example, answers to general questions that can be found by other means (e.g., length of time in business, number of stores, locations of stores) should be known before the meeting. Published articles in newspapers, magazines, and trade publications as well as internet research (see rab.com, tvb.org and onetvworld.org) may provide additional insight as to the challenges and opportunities facing the prospect's industry or a specific company. Conversations with managers, employees and customers will often provide a different perspective than that of an owner or marketing director, who may be a bit removed from the day-to-day operations.

A physical survey will help you develop a first impression of a business and develop recommendations for improvement...from a potential customer's perspective. Is the atmosphere inviting? Are the employees responsive, courteous and helpful when you first walk in? Is the store well merchandised? How is the merchandise displayed? Are they busy? What does a typical customer look like to you? What recommendations would you make from a consumer point of view? Be honest with yourself and with your client about areas in need of improvement. While you may help drive traffic, if they are not prepared to take care of the customers, the customers will not return.

Of course you will always want to know as much personal information about the client as possible (birthdays, family life, hobbies, favorite sports team(s), etc.), but it is absolutely imperative that by the time you leave, you have uncovered the major challenges that the client is facing in his or her business so you can come back with recommended solutions.

Seek first to understand—then to be understood.
-Stephen R. Covey – author, speaker and consultant

WHO ARE THEIR CUSTOMERS?

One of the first things you should ask your prospect is to describe their typical customer. If prompting is needed, you will want to find out if the company attracts more men or more women. Are their products or services used/requested more by people in a particular age range? Are their customers primarily ethnic or non-ethnic? You can make your own assessments regarding these questions by visiting the locations and interviewing company employees, but the information you gather should always be verified by your contact.

This information will help you out in a couple of ways. First, it will let you know if the target profile of your station or programs fits the typical profile of your prospect's clientele. If it does not, you might make the sale one time, but your credibility will be lost if the campaign does not work (which it probably won't), and your chances of landing follow-up sales will be "slim and none."

Secondly, it might also shed light on a different potential customer base that is not being well served. For example, a hardware store that would typically attract a predominately male clientele may want to offer home improvement seminars targeted to women. An auto repair shop that traditionally targets males may want to become more female friendly. A nightclub may want to consider an alcohol-free night geared toward a youth clientele on a Sunday night in the summers when they are ordinarily closed. While every idea may not be feasible, the business owner will appreciate your creative thinking to help maximize the company's resources.

**Our clients do not care about reaching demos;
they care only about reaching customers.**

WHO IS THEIR COMPETITION?

In this age of consolidation, competition is fiercer than ever before. Banking companies offer insurance, insurance companies offer financial services and cellular phone services are encroaching on traditional telephone companies' customer base. Traditional lines of competition are now blurred. The bottom line is that Wall Street demands growth, and every company in every industry is exploring every opportunity to increase its bottom line through growth.

One way to grow is through expansion, but expansion is becoming increasingly difficult as saturation and oversupply limit real growth opportunities. Retail developers continue to develop, despite seeing feasibility studies that show that there is an over-demand in many sectors. Fast-food companies are challenged to find new sites that do not take away from the customer base of their existing outlets.

Another way to grow quickly is through acquisition. National banking companies have consolidated to capture new locations and an existing customer base. However, once expansion is complete, the focus shifts to growth of "same store sales." In an overbuilt market, either the market population has to grow to meet the increasing supply of goods and services or growth has to come from competition (inside and outside the traditional market).

The biggest challenge that today's businesses face is the competition for "share of mind" and for "share of time." Each day we are faced with literally thousands of different messages at every turn. From television, radio, newspaper, billboards, busboards, the internet, direct mail and storefronts there is no escaping the positioning to get our "share of mind." Nonetheless, the biggest competition for our dollars is for "share of time." An available Saturday afternoon may be spent at the mall, at the movies, at a sporting event, at a museum or at home with a video. While none of these venues would consider any of the others a direct competitor, they actually do compete with each other for an individual's mind, time and money.

Too often, companies underestimate their competition and overestimate their customers' loyalty. The reality is that every business has competition, and if it does not, and it is successful, it soon will. Every day, new companies, new products and new services are being launched to chip away at your client's market share.

So what does all this mean to the broadcasting industry? With consolidation, it could mean fewer national players spending fewer advertising dollars. When Wachovia and First Union combined, they spent a considerable amount of money marketing the merger, but their total advertising budget will probably end up being less than what it would have been had they remained individual banks.

There is actually a silver lining in all this for broadcasters. With consolidation come new strategic opportunities for local companies to promote their benefits. Local banks can promote their local roots, exceptional customer service and community commitment. Also, after consolidation and expansion have run their course, the emphasis shifts to increasing same store sales. With so much competition now in every field the only way to increase consumers' "share of mind" and "share of time" is through marketing and advertising. You can be a valued resource to help businesses accomplish their goals.

Competition for the heart, mind and time precedes competition for the money.

IDENTIFY THEIR STRENGTHS, WEAKNESSES, CHALLENGES AND OPPORTUNITIES

In his book *Up Against the Wal-Marts* Don Taylor suggests that you can compete against the major national players, just not at their own game. While it may be difficult, if not impossible, to compete on price or even selection with Wal-Mart, they will never be able to compete on customer service. Nordstrom's "value" is not based on offering the lowest prices, but on their selection of quality merchandise and on their exceptional customer service. 7-Eleven's value comes strictly from convenience, obviously, because their selection is extremely limited and their pricing certainly is not the draw.

Starbucks is a case example of a company that took a commodity product and transformed it into a premium product. It is the quality of the coffee and the quality of the customer experience that creates Starbuck's value. The service is not particularly fast, and a cup of coffee is by no means cheap, but no one can dispute Starbuck's successful formula.

All across the country, national and regional players in every industry are squeezing the "local guys." Increased buying power and national marketing budgets are reducing operating margins in just about every industry. The local players must be realistic in determining their strengths, weaknesses, challenges and opportunities. They must identify and vigilantly promote their unique selling proposition in order to compete. To help your clients determine their unique strengths, you should help them discover why their customers patronize their businesses. Is it the quality of the merchandise, the vast selection, their pricing, their speed or their customer service that stands out? Once you know what it is, develop creative campaigns to promote the strength(s) (without using the obvious clichés).

Also, be honest with your clients about their weaknesses. Are the weaknesses fundamental problems outside of their immediate control (bad location, poor facility, hidden signage, etc.) or is there room for improvement? For the latter, they will probably appreciate your honest assessment along with suggestions of ways to improve. Help them to overcome or minimize the effects of their weaknesses through promotion.

Are there new competitive challenges encroaching on their market share? If not, there probably soon will be, and you should help them prepare by solidifying their current market position. Are there current opportunities that have not been capitalized on or future opportunities that have not been recognized and planned for? When you start identifying new revenue opportunities that have not been previously considered, you will win customers for life.

When you can successfully promote your strengths, deal with your weaknesses, overcome your challenges and capitalize on your opportunities, business is easy.

WHAT IS THEIR PERCEIVED VALUE?

Too often we get caught up in trying to create an immediate need for our client's products and services by promoting weekend sales, special purchase offerings or some other "act now" calls-to-action. While this approach can be extremely effective in the short run for seasonal closeouts or for short-term advertisers, this advertising strategy can be detrimental for long-term advertisers unless they are committed to being a promotional sales account (sale-of-the-week business).

Value is not about having the lowest price. Value is all about the price you pay relative to the expectation of the price you thought you would/should pay. If you go out to a five-star restaurant and end up with a $100 bill that's a great value if your perception was that it was a $200 dinner. Likewise, if you go to a fast-food restaurant where the burger is small and the fries are cold, even a $3 charge is a bad value.

There is a difference between getting what you believe is a *good deal* and getting a *good value*. We once bought an off-brand refrigerator for a few hundred dollars less than the price of the name brand item. We thought we had bought a "good deal," but that was simply a short-term view. A few years later, the hinges started coming off one by one and the drawers stopped functioning properly. A salesman should have sold us on the name brand (even at a higher price), explaining that the lower-priced refrigerator was not a good long term-value. We are now dissatisfied customers that will not patronize that establishment again.

Where are your clients on the "value scale" (from the customers' points of view)? If the pricing is high and there is nothing special about the quality, service, selection or convenience, the perceived value will not be very high and there is little that your campaign can to do to change that. However, if a client offers an exceptional overall customer experience, even at a little higher price, they can still be competitive in the marketplace.

On a scale of 1-5 (one being lowest and 5 being highest), ask your clients where they see themselves relative to others in their industry. Do you agree with their assessment of value (from a customer's perspective) the same way they do? If not, there may be a "perception" problem.

VALUE SCALE

Low————————PRICING—————————High

Low——————— QUALITY—————————High

Low—————————SERVICE—————————High

Low—————————SELECTION—————————High

Low—————————CONVENIENCE———————High

Low————————————VALUE—————————High

Value is determined by the individual consumer. Successful companies consistently provide a lot of value to a lot of individual consumers, over and over again.

UNDERSTAND THE BUYING CYCLES FOR YOUR CLIENT'S PRODUCTS AND SERVICES

While we buy things "unthinkingly" every day, there is a subconscious process that takes place every time a person makes a purchase. This decision-reaching process, or "buying cycle," is generally shorter for impulse items and usually much longer for bigger-ticket items or for more sophisticated purchases. In addition, with the almost overwhelming number of new choices in every product category, buying cycles may be extended because of sheer confusion over what would have been a much simpler decision in year's past.

There are many different interpretations of buying cycles. The AIDA (Attention/Interest/Desire/Action) model first promoted by E.K. Strong in 1925 is still used extensively today. As the years progressed, many others have added steps and different interpretations to the stages that precede a purchase. Below is an adaptation of the Everett Rogers' model, that I believe best describes the steps you go through before making a buy.

AWARENESS – Through marketing, promotion, advertising, PR or word of mouth

INTEREST/INFORMATION – If there is interest, the consumer will seek additional information

EVALUATION – How does the product, service or company compare against existing alternatives?

TRIAL – Could be a trial sample or some other form of a one-time shot to give the new product, service or company a chance

PURCHASE – Involves the purchase, repeat purchase or continued use of a product, service or company

POST PURCHASE EVALUATION – The consumer seeks assurance of the wisdom (value) of the purchase

There may be times that *interest* will preceed *awareness*, and that a consumer will seek out information on a product or service once there is demand. Advertising will be especially important to reach this *new buyer*. Ask your prospect or client what a "typical" buying cycle is for their products or services. Try to identify how long a person will spend in each stage. Is there anything that can be changed or added that could make a decision to purchase easier or quicker (research, testimonials, guarantees, etc.)?

I Still Haven't Found What I'm Looking For
-U2
(Bono lost somewhere in the buying cycle)

12. HOW TO SET GOALS FOR YOUR CLIENTS

UNCOVER THEIR BASELINE SALES

In my early years in the business, Michael Corbett trained me to understand that if you are going to make an objective determination of the success of a marketing campaign, you need to establish baselines numbers from which to begin. Your client can help you begin by providing insight to the following questions.

1) WHAT IS THEIR AVERAGE SALE?

While most companies have a combination of low-ticket sales and high-ticket sales, over a period of time they will establish an average sale. I once worked with a jewelry store owner who said he did not have an average sale. He relayed that a sale could be a $30 Cross pen or a $10,000 engagement ring. I explained to him that he *did* have an average sale, and that it would be his total sales for the year divided by his total number of transactions. For example, if he had annual sales totaling $1,000,000 from 4,000 transactions, his average sale would be $250.

2) WHAT IS THEIR AVERAGE PROFIT PER SALE?

As earlier stated, every business has its "fixed costs," (rent, full-time staff wages, insurance, etc.) that are paid by the company month in and month out, regardless of sales volume. They also have "variable costs," (cost of goods sold, commissions, etc.) which depend upon sales volume. For the purpose of determining ROI on a marketing investment, the difference between the price a product or service is sold for and the variable costs associated with that sale is called the "average profit per sale."

3) WHAT ARE THEIR BASELINE SALES?

This is a sensitive issue, as most business owners do not typically want to share these numbers—unless they trust your confidentiality and truly believe that you can make a difference. If you ask the right questions in your CNA, you can often work backwards to determine these figures on your own. For example, after obtaining the estimated daily traffic, the average ticket and the number of days the business was open for a hair salon chain, I did some quick math to determine that they did around $2,000,000 in annual sales. The owner confirmed that the number was about $50,000 too high, but it was close.

Confidence and confidentiality build credibility.

HELP CLIENTS MAXIMIZE THEIR TRIGGERS FOR GROWTH

In today's business environment, everyone is trying to do more with less. Business owners are stretched in dealing with the day-to-day operations (attracting and managing employees, managing inventory, managing cash flow, etc.). As a result, it is often difficult for them to step outside the trees (product) and see the forest (marketing).

As a marketing partner, you can look at an operation from the outside and help the client determine how to maximize revenue without incurring significant expenses. You should strive to identify every potential profit trigger within the business and determine if there is a way to help maximize the company's potential. The more successful your ideas are in promoting growth, the more you will be counted on for your expertise and the more you will stand out from your competitors, who will still be out there peddling spots.

Every business wants to grow, but not every business has a strategy for achieving that desired growth. There are a number of different "profit triggers" that can help clients achieve their goals. For example, if a client has a goal to increase sales by 20% how is it going to happen? What percentage of that growth will be from new business and what percentage from increased average tickets or from increased frequency of visits per customer? After establishing a baseline value for each trigger, help the client establish a "mini-goal" for each one, along with corresponding strategies for achieving those goals.

The profit triggers will obviously be different depending on the industry. As a media rep, your value will be enhanced if you can help provide creative solutions focused on various triggers rather than just on media placement. The following examples of profit triggers are followed by discussions of issues and strategies related to maximizing each area:

Increase the...

- Number of prospects/shoppers
- Conversion rate of a prospect/shopper to a customer
- Average ticket
- Frequency of visits
- Revenue opportunities within their business
- Number of customer referrals
- Lifetime of a customer

Profit in business comes from repeat customers, customers that boast about your product or service and brings friends with them.
-W. Edward Deming, author and consultant

1) HELP INCREASE THE NUMBER OF THEIR PROSPECTS/SHOPPERS

What would be the financial impact of a clothing retailer increasing the number of shoppers who enter the store from an average of 100 per day to 120 per day? How much more could a temporary staffing company in need of nurses grow by receiving an additional 5 lead calls per day? New business development is always needed for sustained growth, and as a marketing professional, you are relied on for your expertise in this area. By helping to develop a cost-effective marketing plan, you should be able to help your clients increase the number of prospects calling or visiting their locations.

2) HELP INCREASE THE CONVERSION RATE OF A PROSPECT/SHOPPER TO A CUSTOMER

What would happen if a health club could sign up 4 out of 10 prospects who tour the facility instead of their average of 3? What if they could increase the number to 5 or 6 out of 10? While the goal of advertising is to generate lead calls or visits to a prospect's door, it is usually up to the business to convert the increased traffic into increased sales. Therefore, it may possible that the advertising works (i.e., generates traffic), but the return on investment does not materialize.

At one radio station where I worked, I once developed a campaign for a dentist to promote a product called BrightSmile. The cost of this particular treatment was $500. The dentist's variable costs were $200 for the product and $50 for the technician who administered the treatment, leaving him a $250 profit per application. A monthly investment of $1,500 in an advertising campaign would have to generate a minimum of 6 new treatments per month to begin to realize a return of his investment (break even).

We had our midday personality brighten her teeth with the BrightSmile, believing that her live testimonials would relay first hand the difference the treatment made in her smile (without sounding like a typical commercial). After the first month of the campaign, the dentist had received only three sign ups, yet he had received over 60 inquiries. As he and I discussed the situation further, he said that the major obstacle for people was the high price, so a payment plan schedule was put in place. This helped to overcome price as an objection. However, after the program ran, he found out that for calls referred to the

BrightSmile 800 number, the average conversion rate is as high as 20%. If he could have generated this rate of conversion, the campaign would have generated twelve sales, worth $3,000, providing a 100% return on his investment.

3) HELP INCREASE THEIR AVERAGE TICKET

The fast-food industry has perfected the maximization of this profit trigger. McDonald's window servers used to be well trained to ask, "Would you like fries with that?" after taking every order. This subtle suggestive selling technique could increase the total order by over 30%. Even if only every third customer said yes, it would still make for a nice increase in business. Most fast-food chains have now instituted "value meals" to encourage the purchase of fries and a drink with every order. In searching for ways to further increase the average ticket, the fast-food industry also followed up with "super-size" options where for a nominal increase in price, you receive a larger portion of fries or a larger drink.

Increasing the average ticket is partly a function of "the offer" and partly a function of "sales." Great clothing retailers are able to sell a nice shirt and a belt to a customer who comes in for a pair of pants. Best Buy always offers its customers the option of purchasing extended warranties on the products they purchase. Blockbuster offers popcorn to accompany movie rentals. Automotive dealerships offer a host of financing options as well as extended bumper-to-bumper warranties. Some even offer the option to purchase life insurance that will pay off the car loan in the event of the owner's death.

Develop the habit of looking at your client's business objectively and trying to see what program could be put in place to increase the average ticket. Even a 10% average increase translates into a $100,000 gain for a business with $1,000,000 in annual sales. I once set up an incentive program for a hair salon chain to help increase product sales by their stylists. There is no better forum to showcase the benefits of hair care products than in a salon by professional stylists— it's just that most stylists are not trained (or encouraged) to sell. I offered a radio station prize pack (CD's, restaurant certificates, movie tickets, etc.) to the top-selling stylists. Product sales increased immediately, thereby increasing the average ticket for the salon chain.

4) HELP INCREASE THEIR FREQUENCY OF VISITS

A major goal of every business has always been to promote customer loyalty. Early loyalty programs in the mid-20th century included Raleigh cigarette coupons and S&H Green Stamps. With the S&H Green Stamps program, according to the amount of their purchase supermarket customers would earn a certain number of green stamps, which they then could redeem for various types of merchandise.

American Airlines revolutionized the airline industry in 1981 with a customer loyalty program called the AAdvantage. Given comparable pricing, comparable scheduling and comparable service, why wouldn't passengers fly with an airline that would let them earn mileage credits for a free trip? It was such a good idea that within days United began their own frequent flier program called Mileage Plus. Later that same year Delta and TWA followed suit. Now according to Frequentflier.com there are an estimated 70 frequent flier programs worldwide with over 100 million members. After many years of not having such a program and realizing that other airlines were siphoning away their business customers, even Southwest Airlines finally began offering a program of their own.

Following the airlines' lead, other industries quickly followed suit with rewards programs for their frequent customers. Holiday Inn was the first in the hotel industry to launch their program in January of 1983 and Marriott followed suit later that same year. Now most every category of retail has its own type of rewards program. Originally, frequent-visit punch cards would offer a free product or service—bagel, car wash, dry cleaning, whatever—after a specified number of visits. In most businesses these wallet cards have now been replaced by scanned rewards cards issued by grocery stores, office supply stores, drug stores, malls, and a host of specialty retailers. The number of participating retailers is so high that many people now have separate key rings just for their loyal customer cards. Starbucks created the Starbucks card, which offers its frequent customers the convenience of not having to mess with cash or credit cards, thereby increasing the frequency of visits.

Work with each of your clients to find out, on average, how many purchases per year (occasions) the average customer makes. For example, a restaurant's average patron may visit six times a year; an average hair care shop patron may average twelve times a year; a typical automotive service shop customer might visit three times a year. Determine what could be offered to increase the frequency by just one or two additional times per year. Do your clients have customer loyalty programs in place? Can they have private pre-season sales twice a year for their VIP Club members and promote to their customers via email?

5) HELP INCREASE REVENUE OPPORTUNITIES WITHIN THEIR BUSINESS

There are two ways to increase profits: one is to increase revenue (top line) and the other is to decrease operating expenses. You need to discover whether your clients have additional profit centers available outside of their traditional customer or distribution base. Alltel, a cellular phone service provider, found a new profit center by setting up kiosks in retailer's locations that have nothing to do with electronics or telecommunications, but—-they have floor traffic. In addition to providing a new revenue source for Alltel, this arrangement provided new revenue opportunities for retailers with available floor space to rent—-it's a win-win situation.

The Applebee's, Chile's and Red Robin restaurant chains are now promoting their "take out" service to capitalize on what pizza and Chinese restaurants have known for years: many people do not like to cook, but don't have time to sit down to order a meal at a restaurant. These traditional sit-down restaurants have the kitchen, cooks and other necessary personnel, so why not maximize the utilization of their resources?

Can you identify additional revenue opportunities that will help your clients grow their businesses? Are there new markets that have not been considered? Are there new distribution channels that could impact their sales? Are there co-promotional possibilities with other station clients? When you identify new revenue opportunities for your clients, you are sure to get more sales opportunities in return.

6) HELP INCREASE THEIR NUMBER OF REFERRALS

If you ask most people in business to name their best source of advertising, they probably would say "word-of-mouth." Once, while training a group of radio reps, I asked what hair stylists they (a mix of both men and women) used. Seven of the reps mentioned the same small shop and the same stylist within that shop. As I probed further, I found that one person "discovered" the stylist and recommended her to two other co-workers, who then each referred the stylist to two others in the organization. At an average charge of $30 per visit and 12 visits per year, the average yearly value to that stylist was $360 per person. Therefore, the referral value of the other six people in the organization was $2,160 per year. These reps had been seeing this stylist for an average of three years, so the lifetime value of this one person's referral was $6,480 at the time of our training session. The best part about it is that this was *free advertising*!

While most successful businesses rely, to a degree, on word-of-mouth advertising, few actually have programs set up to encourage word-of-mouth exposure. With all due respect to the media, few commercials can be as effective in transferring the confidence to try a restaurant, stay at a hotel or see a new play as the recommendation by a friend.

American Family Fitness, a successful health club chain

in Richmond, Virginia, has posters throughout all of their clubs saying, "Refer a friend!" This chain offers different incentives throughout the year to those members who bring in referrals who join. It may be a free one-month membership, American Family Fitness gym bags or sweatshirts. Their goal is to keep top-of-mind awareness for their referral program- and it works!

Consider what type of programs could be used to "incent" word-of-mouth advertising for your customers. If you are working with an oil change/quick lube establishment, would it be worth a free oil change as an incentive for giving a good referral? If one person recommends three new customers and receives three free oil changes, it might cost an establishment $50 out-of-pocket, but those three new customers could be worth thousands of dollars if they become satisfied customers for life. Remember, the more you can help your clients increase their business, the more budget they will have available for you with outside marketing.

7) HELP INCREASE THEIR LIFETIME OF A CUSTOMER

How long does an average customer patronize your client's business? Is it one year, three years or five years? Do they stop coming because they are lured by a competitor's special or were they dissatisfied with their last visit and never bothered to say anything before they walked out the door? There will always be uncontrollable factors that result in defections (relocation, aging out of the target market, etc.) but most customer attrition can be prevented, thereby extending the average lifetime of a customer.

Too often, advertisers believe that an advertising campaign is unsuccessful when the investment exceeds the "initial" return. If a $5,000 hair salon chain promotion generates fifty new customers at a $30 average ticket, the "initial" return would be $1,500. However, if just half of this group were to be converted to long-term customers, the annual value of this new client base could be $9,000 (if they visited once a month).

Help your prospects and clients see the "lifetime value of a customer." You may need your client to provide you with information. For example, if you are working with a health club chain with four metro locations, you will need to know a few facts before you can start making calculations.

QUESTIONS:

Q: What is your average monthly membership fee? $50

Q: How many years does a typical member stay with your club?   2

Q: What percentage of your business comes from referrals?   33%

SUMMARY:

The average annual membership value is: $600

The lifetime value of one member would be (2 years): $1,200

Therefore the lifetime value of a customer (including referrals) would be: $1,596

($1,200 x .33 + $1,200)

Obviously with different industries, you have to rephrase the questions to fit each particular situation. For companies with product sales, for example, you need to know the gross profit per transaction (average ticket less cost of goods sold). In working with a restaurant, you might collect the following data and calculate the associated figures.

QUESTIONS:

Q: What is your average meal transaction charge per customer?   **$60**

Q: What is the gross profit per transaction (transaction charge less food cost)?   **$38 (63%)**

Q: How many times per year does your average patron eat at your restaurant?   **4**

Q: How many years does an average customer patronize your restaurant?   **4**

Q: What percentage of your business comes from referrals?   **25%**

SUMMARY:

The average annual value of a customer is ($38 profit per visit x 4 visits):   **$152**

The lifetime value of one customer is ($152 x 4 years):   **$608**

The lifetime value of a customer, including their corresponding referrals is: **$760**

($608 x .25 + $608)

Helping your clients see the long-term value of advertising will help you in framing expectations of the campaign. You should verify any numbers that you generate with your prospect to make sure that your values are in line. If they are not, use input from the client to make the adjustments needed until you get agreement.

13. HOW TO POSITION YOUR CLIENT'S BUSINESS

HELP THEM BUILD AN EQUITY POSITION IN THE MARKETPLACE

As earlier stated, Michael Corbett, in his book *33 Ruthless Rules of Advertising*, defines an "equity position" in the context of advertising as "when people think of your business when they have a need for the product or service that you sell." In the world of groceries, shoe stores and hardware stores, what companies in your local market come to mind? If you have preferred stores that you frequently visit, they will probably be the first names that come to mind, and some form of advertising probably triggered your first visit.

What about categories of business that sell products or services that you do not typically use regularly or shop around for, but that you may someday have a need for? What company names come to mind when you think of attorneys or auto insurance? What is your impression of these companies, having never been a client? If it is favorable, you are likely to give them first consideration when the need arises.

Typically, it is the branding through advertising that will

create these "top-of-mind" impressions. The companies that have made the up-front marketing investment to stand out from their competition will reap the rewards on the backside. Since most companies are dealing with finite marketing budgets, it is more important for a company to brand itself to a smaller market first, but to do so with frequency (each week) and consistency (multiple weeks) to build awareness. You can help your clients build their equity position with your morning program viewers or your afternoon drive show listeners. Chances are the cume (potential weekly audience) viewership or listenership will be more than sufficient to make a difference in their business. As budget permits and awareness is built, you can expand the audience to dominate other time periods with consistency.

If you are not known for being something to someone, you will be known for nothing to no one.

HELP THEM PROMOTE (OR CREATE) THEIR UNIQUE SELLING PROPOSITION (USP)

Jack Welch, former CEO of General Electric, once said, "If you don't have a competitive advantage, you shouldn't compete." An expanded quote should add that, "If you have a competitive advantage but do not promote it to your prospects, you *will not compete.*" Every business should be known for something.

In his book *Ogilvy on Advertising*, David Ogilvy suggests the best way to beat P&G is, of course, to market a better product." Many of your prospects and your clients believe they have a better product (or service). The problem is that many of their potential customers do not know what it is or why it is better. If a company does not promote and continually reinforce its competitive advantage, the competition will win.

Since the 1990's the Westin hotel chain has been known for their Heavenly Beds, which included a mix of pillow-top mattresses, down comforters and pillows, and a crisp white duvet. This innovation was the result of identifying the unique needs, wants and desires of their customers and delivering a product to satisfy these needs, wants and desires. Not only did this effort help turn around the Westin brand, by increasing customer loyalty, the company says that 30,000 customers have bought one of the beds from Westin. Now every major hotel chain is following Westin's lead with new bedding programs of their own. Marriott announced in early 2005 that it is buying 628,000 beds to replace nearly every bed in its seven-hotel chain.

A company's Unique Selling Proposition (USP) should include a tagline or catch phrase that is included with the company name in all commercial messages and in all promotional literature. An example of messages with different intentions can be found in the insurance industry. While most full-service insurance companies offer similar products, some want to be known for their "financial strength," such as Prudential (Get a Piece of the Rock) and Pacific Life (Rely on the Strength of Pacific Life). Others want to be known for their "caring attitude." Nationwide (Is on Your Side), Allstate (You're in Good Hands) and State Farm (Like a Good Neighbor) want you to feel a big group hug when you watch their commercials.

AFLAC had one of the most successful branding campaigns in history designed to overcome an unfamiliar name with the introduction of the AFLAC duck. Their tagline, "Ask for it at work," is designed to stimulate an action.

On a local level, you can be a part of helping to develop a client's USP. When I was an account executive, Michael Corbett was consulting with our station and we worked with a company called The Ice House. The problem was that their name did not clearly identify their business. It could have been a nightclub or a company that sold ice, when, in fact, it was an ice-skating rink. While the owner truly believed that he had no competition, since there were no other ice rinks in the surrounding area, we explained to him that the venue faced competition from other entertainment venues, including movie theaters, bowling alleys and miniature golf facilities. A USP was needed to differentiate the business from these other entertainment options.

When the owner was asked why people go ice-skating, the word "fun" in some form or another continually emerged in his responses. He felt that The Ice House offered "a fun alternative" to other traditional entertainment venues. We followed this lead and came up with the tagline, "Put your fun on ice—at the Ice House." To accentuate the ice-skating experience for the radio listener, we took a tape recorder to the rink and recorded a sudden stop "Shhhhhhhhhhhhhhhk!" to insert after the words, "put your fun on ice." We suggested that he use this tagline in everything he did to reinforce the message.

Spend some time helping your prospects and clients define

what they want to be known for. Talk to their company employees to get a diversity of input on what attracts the public to their business. Then interview their customers and ask why they shop there or use the services provided. Break it down to a brief and memorable slogan that communicates their competitive advantage.

Make sure that your Unique Selling Proposition translates to a customer's unique buying advantage (why would they want to buy from you?).

HELP YOUR CLIENTS "WIN THE LOVE" OF THEIR CUSTOMERS

The "customer experience" is more than the use of a commoditized product or service. Kevin Roberts, CEO of Saatchi and Saatchi Worldwide, suggests that it should create a long-term emotional connection with consumers. People do not need thousands of different choices; they just need the one choice that meets their personal needs.

Roberts believes that branding has run its course. In his book *The Future Beyond Brands—Lovemarks,* he explains that recognition of brands is no longer good enough. The "moment of truth" comes when a consumer faces the decision of which company to call, what retailer to visit or which product to pick off the shelf. It is the company (or product) that has a special place in the hearts and minds of the consumers that will form the bonds that create customers for life.

Do your clients have that "loyalty beyond reason" with

their customers? Do they use mystery, sensuality and inti-
macy that Roberts suggest using to create "Lovemarks" with
consumers?   While "branding" deals more with the mind
(top-of-mind, share-of-mind, etc.), go straight for the heart
when promoting your client's products and services.

All You Need is Love
-The Beatles

14. HOW TO CREATE A MARKETING CAMPAIGN

DETERMINANTS OF CAMPAIGN SUCCESS

When it comes down to it, three primary variables determine the effectiveness of a media campaign:

1. The appropriateness of the station or programs
2. The schedule (impact, domination and frequency)
3. The message (compelling copy/presentation that sells)

If the station or program does not reach a desired potential clientele, chances are the schedule or message will not matter. If the schedule is not designed for impact, domination and frequency, the message will not be heard enough to make a meaningful difference. And finally, if the commercial message does not influence buying behavior, the campaign will not succeed.

Imagine all the people—walking through your door.
-Lennon/Guld

THE APPROPRIATENESS OF THE STATION OR PROGRAMS

The reality is that most every radio or television station has enough listeners and viewers to provide results for a client.

Another reality is that most programming is designed to reach a targeted clientele. On the television side, Monday Night Football will primarily attract one type of audience and Oprah will attract another. On the radio side, an Alternative Rock format will attract a different audience than a Hip Hop station or an Oldies station.

Most media outlets do not succeed by being all things to all people. They target their programming (and consequently, attract advertising) to "superserve" the tastes of viewers and listeners primarily by age, sex and race. All of this is not to say that women do not watch football or that men do not watch Oprah. However, it does mean that you would be hard-pressed to find a Clinique commercial during a football game or a Budweiser commercial during Oprah.

What is your station's dominant age cell (usually defined by no more than a 20-year span)? What percentage of your listeners are male and what percentage are female? Does your station primarily attract an ethnic or a white audience? Does your station skew more toward listeners with higher incomes or those with lower incomes? While there seems to be a desire to portray only upscale viewers and listeners, those in the middle and on the other end of the socioeconomic spectrum have their markets as well.

While statistics related to the questions above can easily be attained, it is best to bring your audience to life for your prospects. For example, if your television station is having a live guest appearance of one of your nationally syndicated guest hosts, invite your prospect to attend the event to see their potential shoppers. If your radio station is putting on a concert, festival or station promotion, invite prospects and clients to the event and show off their potential clientele. At a very minimum, capture these events on video and take a lot of "crowd pictures" to use in your marketing.

You must be careful not to over-target. Mass media is obviously not as targeted as direct mail. However, the key criterion is to determine if the average profile of your station or station programs fits the average profile of your prospect's target clientele. If it does not, your selling skills may help you make an initial sale, but the lack of results that will probably ensue will not help you build a customer for life.

There are hundreds to thousands of potential prospects in a given market. If you do a little research and prospect only those accounts that are most appropriate for your station, everyone wins in the long run.

Know your target; grow from your target.

15. HOW TO HELP YOUR CLIENTS BUDGET FOR GROWTH

ADVERTISING BUDGETS WERE MADE TO BE BROKEN

While most small business owners set advertising budgets as a part of their overall budgets, these budgets are likely to be more flexible than those of national corporations. If a sensible opportunity to increase their business is presented, the owner of a small business might decide to "bust the budget," depending on their estimated ROI.

Make no mistake about it: most business owners are not sitting in their offices waiting around for the next media rep to walk in the door to claim their portion of an unused advertising budget. They are getting multiple calls every day from people pitching their newspapers, magazines, billboards, community shoppers, and direct mail pieces as well as by radio and television station reps. It makes sense that the more visible and successful a business is, the more advertising calls it will get. In addition, the internet has proven itself as a viable competitor to brick-and-mortar retailers. It will continue to siphon more advertising dollars away from traditional media in the years to come.

With all this competition, how do you talk to business owners and have them seriously consider your opportunity?

You need to talk their language and talk about the only thing they really care about—return on investment (ROI). At the end of the day (or at the end of the campaign) all they really care about is how much return they realized on their investments. I have even experimented with "guaranteeing results" or guaranteeing a return *of* their investment over a period of time, committing to run the campaign at the quoted cost until the guarantee is met. While I have been successful in enticing new business that otherwise would not have been on the station, it takes a true trusting partnership to venture in this direction. Unfortunately, with the intangible nature of the broadcast medium, it is usually too subjective and too difficult to venture in this arena.

By focusing on setting goals for the campaign, you can steer the conversation away from concern about the "advertising budget." Help your prospects and clients to see that it is more about the "opportunity cost," or the potential loss of revenue by not doing the campaign. I have even framed the investment decision in very simple terms by asking clients, "If you give me $5,000 and I give you back $7,500 in return (figures can vary), would you do it?" Most all agree that they would. The next question I ask is: "*Could* you do it? (that is, would they have the funds?)" If their answer is yes, then you have something to talk about.

The bottom line is that there has to be a correlation between the advertising budget and the anticipated results of a campaign. Typically, the greater the budget, the greater the reach (number of stations, number of weeks, number of dayparts/programs, etc.), and as a result, the greater the anticipated returns. Conversely, an advertiser who can afford only a limited number of commercials over a limited number of weeks should adjust his expectations of results accordingly.

Perceived value creates discretionary budgets.

WHAT IS YOUR CLIENT'S ANTICIPATED RETURN ON INVESTMENT (ROI)?

Determining an anticipated return on investment (ROI) from marketing is difficult for most advertising reps (as well as for the clients they are working with). It is an area that is rarely discussed in advance of a campaign and rarely considered after its completion. Not having clear expectations makes it difficult to get a meaningful measure of the results of a campaign.

How do you know what the ROI of a marketing campaign should be? You have to start by knowing where the client would have been had you never walked in the door. Clients usually have baseline sales figures that they use along with information on sales trends to give them a pretty good idea of where they are going to be, assuming all other factors stay the same. Therefore, the growth that can be attributed to your campaign should be the difference between the results you help them achieve and their anticipated results before your involvement.

For example, if a company has been growing an average of 5% per year over the past three years, it is a good bet that they will grow in the 5% range next year, assuming everything else stays the same. If you can help them grow by 7% next year, the additional 2% should be credited to your efforts.

It is best to determine in advance (in your CNA) what the expected ROI is for a client. Is he or she expecting a 20% ROI or a 200% ROI? Sometimes, those projected numbers can seem too large and distant to truly comprehend, so the first thing to discuss with local advertisers is "Return *of* Investment." Determine the number of sales that would be required to offset the proposed marketing expense. At that point, the campaign will have at least paid for itself, not to mention the additional exposure and potential long-term benefits generated by the promotion.

You will then want to know what the true expectations are for a minimum return *on* investment. Simply put, for every $1,000 invested in a campaign, what does the client expect back in return? Determine in your own mind if this number is realistic. It is better to know in advance how the success of your campaign will be judged.

The ROI percentage will probably be determined using input from a number of different variables. What are the estimated returns from other financial investments of similar risk? What have the returns been historically with other marketing campaigns? While everyone would like to double, triple or even quadruple the returns on investments, using too high a benchmark for defining success may lead to perceived failure. Again, it is always better to "under-promise"—-this increases the odds that you will be able to "over-deliver."

As the next step in developing a campaign strategy, it is now time to determine the number of prospects needed for your client to reach the ROI goal. You will need to get five specific pieces of information from your client to help you with your calculations.

Average Ticket - Total sales for a given period divided by the number of transactions

Profit Margin – Average ticket less cost of goods sold divided back by average ticket

Closing Ratio – The percentage of shoppers/prospects that will actually buy

ROI – What is the anticipated return for every dollar invested in advertising?

Number of days open per month

Furniture Store Example:
Suppose you are working with a furniture store that is considering a $14,000 twenty-week advertising investment with you. In your uncovery you have learned that the average ticket is $500 with a 50% profit margin and a closing ratio of 25%. The store is open six days a week and the client expects a 30% "minimum" return on the advertising investment (although they would be extremely satisfied with double that).

ADVERTISING INVESTMENT: $14,000 ($700 per week)	
+ EXPECTED ROI: 30%	$4,200
= RETURN NEEDED (Advertising investment + expected ROI):	$18,200
/ GROSS PROFIT PER TRANSACTION:	$250
= NUMBER OF SALES NEEDED	72.8
/ CLOSING PERCENTAGE	25%
= NUMBER OF TOTAL PROSPECTS NEEDED (14.5 per week or 2.5 per day)	291

If the twenty-week schedule reaches an estimated 75,000 prospects in the target demographic (net reach), you would need to convert .4% of your listeners/viewers to furniture shoppers at the client's store. Is that figure realistic? Ask your prospect if he/she believes it is. Is it possible to reach double that figure to achieve the highest satisfaction level (60% ROI) expressed by the client?

It is here that you can also provide the client with qualitative information to help build your case. If you have research that shows that 25% of your listeners/viewers plan on buying furniture within the next 12 months, you could say that the schedule will be reaching 18,750 "now buyers." Is it realistic that you could direct just 1.6% of your listeners/viewers who plan on buying furniture in the next year to the store to reach the target ROI?

Takin' care of business...every day.
Takin' care of business...every way.
-BTO

16. HOW TO SCHEDULE A CAMPAIGN

SCHEDULING FOR IMPACT

The reason that it is imperative to know the buying cycle for your client's products or services is that the schedule should at least extend through a full buying cycle (or cycles). Otherwise, by the time an individual has a need for a product or service, the schedule may have ended, and other companies will have become "top-of-mind." The proverbial "I'll try advertising for a week and see if it works" will rarely work because it will probably not even make it to the "purchase" phase of the buying cycle.

Once it has been determined that your station or programs have a viewership or listernership base that is attractive to your prospect, the next step is to create an effective schedule. Budget permitting for radio, it is best to dominate the entire station through a version of Optimum Effective Scheduling (OES), a scheduling technique designed to reach the station's core listeners through repeated exposures. It relies on concentration and domination of commercial exposures. The challenge is that few companies have the budget to sustain this type of scheduling with consistency.

Assuming that budget is a consideration, traditional theory has been that it is preferable to maximize the potential audience of a given program, day or daypart before expanding the schedule and adding commercials in other timeslots or during other programs. In other words, it is better to reach 10,000 people effectively (3 or more times) than to have 50,000 people see or hear an ad one time, but not remember it (ineffective exposures). This theory holds especially with the introduction of new companies, new products or new services where repeated exposures are needed to explain their benefits.

Historically, there have been two primary ways to create an effective schedule—horizontally and vertically. Horizontal scheduling allows an advertiser to achieve repetition within a specific time frame each day. For example, a furniture store may sponsor the 7:50 am local newsbreak within the national morning show every weekday. Or perhaps a car dealership may dominate the afternoon every day. As a result, these advertisers will effectively reach viewers and listeners who have the same daily viewing and listening habits.

Even on a limited budget, horizontal scheduling can achieve good results. For example, restaurants looking to build their lunch business could horizontally schedule one commercial just before the lunch hour every day. If a client's budget permits, two or more commercials in the pre-lunch time slot would be even better. Research shows that most lunch decisions are made minutes before pulling into the restaurant. With a compelling message and a *consistent* schedule, the five to ten commercials each week will drive lunch business.

Vertical scheduling is the domination of a day(s) or portions of a day(s). A retailer on a limited budget may choose to dominate Saturdays to generate additional business on the traditionally busiest shopping day of the week. A golf course could dominate Saturday and Sunday mornings to entice viewers or listeners to call for tee times and head out to the links. I once worked with Tanas Hair Design, a single hair salon in Raleigh, North Carolina that wanted to grow but that was on an extremely limited budget. The owner, Jack Tanas, understood the need for domination, frequency and consistency. I placed him on an annual campaign of six commercials back-to-back every Sunday, a day he was not even open. With a creative campaign, he saw great results! He now has multiple locations.

Michael Jordan's RPM Nissan in Durham, North Carolina used to combine the vertical and horizontal scheduling formula by advertising a spot per hour every Wednesday, Thursday and Friday in the afternoon drive on a number of radio stations. Although they usually aired only twelve commercials per week, the targeting of the schedule combined with the consistency of the campaign (each week) made you feel as if the automotive dealership was on all the time.

A relatively new approach to scheduling was developed by Erwin Ephron, a partner with Ephron, Papazian & Ephron, Inc. in New York. A former ad executive, Ephron believes that "it is the events in a person's life—the empty cereal box, the high telephone bill, the broken dishwasher, the expiring car lease – that get consumers to consider making a purchase, not the insistence of advertising messages." Being there with a message when the consumer is ready to buy is the most important thing for successful advertising. Therefore, he advocates "recency planning" with a media goal of reaching "as many different consumers as possible in as many different weeks as possible in order to reach the few that are in the market at any time." His model is based more on "reach and continuity," believing that longer-term schedules (52-week, preferably) are preferred over high-frequency schedules over shorter periods of time.

Regardless of the scheduling theory that you choose to follow, all agree on the need for consistency. Few advertisers will ever achieve long-term success with short-term schedules. Help your clients understand that they did not start their business for a month and see if it works. Like their business, effective advertising takes a commitment.

An outstanding commercial with an ineffective schedule will still produce ineffective results.

YOUR RATES...OUR TERMS; OUR RATES...YOUR TERMS

Everyone likes to feel that they are "getting a good deal." However, in the case of media sales, broadcasters are dealing with a finite inventory. As a result, the "value" of station commercials will be priced by their advertisers through available supply and market demand. Some stations, individual shows or station dayparts with high ratings may have more demand than available supply, leading to higher rates (and lower efficiencies). Conversely, other stations, individual shows or lower-rated dayparts may not have adequate demand and could be left unsold leading to "spoiled inventory" by the next day. In such cases, lower rates may be used to attract revenue that otherwise would be lost.

Rarely are all programs and all dayparts sold out every day. Ken Wayland, a former sales manager once told me his strategy on rates: "Your rates...our terms; our rates...your terms." Translated, this means that clients who pay "market rates" can choose when and where they would like their ads to run. However, clients who care only about "lower rates" can accomplish their goal as long as they are flexible as to when and where their commercials air. They can't have both.

You can't always get what you want.
-The Rolling Stones

17. HOW TO CREATE A COMMERCIAL

WHAT'S THE TAKEAWAY OF THE COMMERCIAL?

As Roy Williams points out, most locally produced commercials focus on the who, what, when and where (as directed by clients' extensive copy points), when the only thing that most consumers really want to know is "Why?"—Why should I change my shopping behavior or even consider a new company product or service?

However, the creative challenge is first to overcome the listener's or viewer's question: "Why should I even stay tuned to the rest of the commercial?" Will I be entertained, informed or enlightened? Is there someone talking to me about something I need or may desire? Is there something that will make my life easier, make me happier or richer or bring me love? Is it something that I am in the market for today? If not, why should I remember the message when the time comes for me to buy? The commercial itself should provide clear answers to these questions.

A "priority problem" in the media sales world is that while hours, days, months and years are spent identifying prospects, gathering contact numbers, making appointments, doing CNA's, presenting proposals, overcoming objections and trying to close sales, typically the smallest percentage of a media rep's time is spent with the conception and creation of the ad.

The fact is that most media sales people prefer the "selling process" over the "creative strategy process," and they usually just want to get the second part over with. Another issue is that most clients do not know what they really want or need, and they rely on the media "experts" to guide them through the process of deciding. The creative strategy is probably the most important determinant for the success or failure of a campaign. When all is said and done, it comes down to that fifteen-, thirty- or sixty-second's worth of air.

If more time were spent on the creative strategy to ensure a more effective campaign, repeat orders would be greater, billing would be higher and reps would need to spend less of their precious time in the selling and reselling process to make up for attrition. The problem is usually not having a comfort zone with the creative process. Few of us were ever really trained on how to create an effective media campaign.

**If you spend more time "creating,"
you won't have to spend as much time "selling."**

WHERE'S THE BEEF?

While I believe the goals of media advertising are to create "share of mind (and heart)" and "share of time," which ultimately should result in a "share of dime (dollars)," there are many different ways these goals can be accomplished. Every advertiser (or person creating the ad) should have an end result in mind before the writing begins. What is the desired "takeaway" of the ad? What is the one point that you want listeners/viewers to remember at the end of the commercial? If you played that commercial to ten people, would the message be clearly understood and consistently repeated by all or could there be various interpretations? It's a good idea to write the message that you want to convey at the top of the page before beginning and then to stay focused on that message throughout the script.

In 1974 McDonalds introduced a campaign to promote The Big Mac by stating all its ingredients in the catchy jingle: "two all-beef patties special sauce lettuce cheese pickles onions on a sesame seed bun." Most baby boomers can still state the ingredients today, many years later. In 1984, Wendy's wanted to dramatize the small size of competing hamburgers and introduced a campaign of commercials with the catch phrase: "Where's the beef?" This campaign effectively positioned the size of Wendy's burgers over those of the competition.

The most successful commercial advertising campaigns identify a core message to be conveyed, develop a campaign theme by which to best convey that message and then stick to it. Sears used the slogan "The Softer Side of Sears" to bring women back to Sears. Chevrolet uses the phrase "Like a Rock" to accentuate the durability of their trucks. Nike encourages the average person to "Just Do It," saying that there is an athlete inside each and every one of us consumers.

I do not regard advertising as entertainment or an art form, but as a medium of information. When I write an advertisement, I don't want you to tell me that you find it "creative"; I want you to find it so interesting that you buy the product.
-David Ogilvy

PULL THE TRIGGER

What is it that can be stated in an ad that will trigger emotional feelings or logical reasoning with your listeners or viewers? You may be tapping into an existing need, want or desire, creating a new need or you may be bringing out a suppressed fear or insecurity. First identify the trigger that you are going to use and then design and focus your campaign around that theme.

Hunger is a natural trigger for restaurants—hence the sight and sound of sizzling steaks in the Applebee's commercials. However, there are quite a few dining options in every market, and once people are in a buying mood, they rely on certain basic criteria to make their buying decisions. For dining decisions, these criteria might include a combination of cuisine, ambience, service, location and price, all of which play a part in the perceived value of the overall dining experience and the selection of where to go.

What is it that motivates a change in perception and a change in buying behavior? Why would someone decide to shop at a local sporting goods store instead of at Dick's Sporting Goods? More than likely, it would not be for a larger selection or a lower price. Is there a desire for more personalized attention that a category killer such as Dick's is unable to provide? Is there a wider selection of quality bicycles for young children? Does the service include customized bicycle fittings and free annual tune ups with all purchases?

Obviously, different people have different buying triggers. When buying a car, some people may place a greater importance on safety, others on style and still others on durability. Yet most dealers go right to promoting lowest price, which forces lower margins and places no value on the other benefits of the dealership (better buying experience, free oil changes with every purchase, computerized service records, free loner car, etc.)

Identify the single trigger that is going to motivate a change in perception and hopefully a change in buying behavior. When you do, build the campaign theme around that trigger.

What you want, (hooo) baby I got it.
What you need, (hooo) you know I got it.
-Aretha Franklin
(pulling the emotional trigger)

DETERMINE THE BEST APPROACH
TO CONVEY THE MESSAGE

Everyone has seen or heard great commercial campaigns. Some are elaborate productions with exceptionally high production costs, and others are simple messages created with great wit. Some use high profile celebrity endorsements, while others are promoted by local afternoon drive personalities. Some commercials make you laugh, and others tug at your emotions. However, the common denominators of all effective promotional campaigns are high "relatedness" and "relevance." Relatedness is a measure of the viewer's or listener's ability to immediately identify, connect or associate with the message. Relevance deals with how pertinent or how meaningful the message is to a viewer or listener at that time.

It is difficult for the typical person to relate to tire tread design or other tire components designed to promote safety. However, the visual image of a baby sitting in a tire in conjunction with the spoken message "You've got a lot riding on your tires" gets viewers every time. With these television commercials Michelin appealed directly to the emotional benefit of safety with a campaign that was extraordinarily relatable and relevant to parents.

Dan O'Day, a respected radio consultant, states that "advertising is not an exercise in creativity—it is mass salesmanship with creativity being the tool." If an ad entertains but does not sell, it does not work. It's not about winning ad awards; it's about winning over the hearts and minds of consumers and motivating them to make a purchase. The first step in this process is keeping listeners and viewers tuned in to your station (both physically and mentally). There are a number of different ways to do this. The following are examples of just a few.

To have a great idea, have a lot of them.
-Thomas Edison

HUMOR

Everyone loves a funny commercial. Millions tune in to the

Super Bowl every year to be entertained by the new Budweiser ads. AFLAC designed humorous campaigns around their duck. Humor can be extremely effective not only in enhancing advertising recall, but also in fueling "buzz," such as water cooler conversation.

Humor is most effective in commercials when it is used to dramatize a point. For example, the tag line of Geico is: "One fifteen-minute call could save you fifteen percent or more." In one television campaign, the company dramatized the excitement of saving money, expressed at inopportune times. One reason humor works for Geico is because the central message is not lost, as it often is in other commercials that may be entertaining, but not effective.

Another caveat is that creating humorous ads is not easy, and a campaign can fail miserably if the humor's relevance does not extend beyond the copywriter or the client to the target audience. Always discuss new campaign concepts with others, and play new commercials to a small test group before releasing the ads to the masses—-just to make sure the humor works. Of course, you must make sure the small test group you choose mirrors the target market. Playing a commercial for your twenty-something-year-old buddies will do little to test its marketing effectiveness if your target market is women in their forties.

Let me just add that you might find yourself having to convince a client that he or she does not have to like the commercial, which can be a difficult task. As an example, owners of video game businesses may not relate well to the humor that the kids who buy the games will relate to.

EMOTION

Will the purchase of a new diamond necklace bring "true love?" Will a new red Corvette convertible bring "midlife happiness?" Commercials that touch an emotional need, want or desire can inspire action. Jewelry stores and cruise ship operators appeal to the positive emotions, such as love, fun, and happiness. Hair replacement and weight-loss companies appeal to consumers' oppressed insecurity and vanity. In other words, their products and services may be sold as ways to overcome negative feelings, such as loneliness and embarrassment.

Other industries use fear (always a great motivator) to trigger purchasing responses in a target audience. Scott Alarm is a dominant alarm company based out of Jacksonville, Florida. Its founder, Bruce Scott, is a former policeman who built a business by using fear as a motivator. His commercials used to revolve around his message: "While you are away on vacation, burglars could be breaking into your house."

Neurologist Donald Calne states that "the essential difference between emotion and reason is that emotion leads to action while reason leads to conclusion." Most of your clients want action.

LOGIC

While appeals to emotions can trigger interest or the impulse to shop, logic may still be needed to convince people to buy. When actually standing in front of the diamond necklace, the consumer might begin to wonder whether the purchase would be a good investment (as if it would ever really be sold, right?)

Perhaps the 45-year-old male, seeking new excitement in life, begins to wonder about the re-sale value of the BMW convertible he is looking at. Oftentimes, the rational justification process may be better addressed in the internal sales process, rather than in outside marketing.

However, for some ads a logical presentation of the benefits that come with a product, service or company, in comparison to what competitors offer, may be the best approach. This is especially true when rational decision-making as opposed to emotional decision-making is guiding the purchase.

Consumers may have any number of questions that they are thinking through at different stages of the "buying cycle." Does the product or service being promoted save time, save aggravation, save money or perhaps even help make you money? How much money will be saved? Can it be proven? Even if a rational approach is chosen, it does not mean that a "rip and read" is acceptable. Your ad still needs to get the attention of your target consumer, relate to them, prove credibility and keep them interested.

TESTIMONIALS

Most business owners will agree that their best form of advertising is word-of-mouth. Most individual consumers will agree that they are more likely to try an unfamiliar restaurant if a friend recommends it. Most of us are naturally skeptical of new places and new things. Hearing good things from others makes us feel better about exploring new territory or trying new products. Television and radio provides word-of-mouth advertising on a mass scale. Testimonials personalize the message even more. When your favorite personality endorses a product or service, your feeling is: "If it's good enough for them, it must be good enough for me."

Have you ever had the experience of meeting a prospect who was so good at describing his or her philosophy and explaining the company's mission and reason for success that you wished you had a tape recorder by your side? The first-hand passion evident in such a situation could never be replicated by a third-party voice "reading the copy." That's the experience I had when I first met with Mark Smith, owner of Midas of Richmond. I pleaded with him to do his own commercials, but he originally resisted, saying he did not care about the ego. I explained that my recommendation had nothing to do with ego and everything to do with results. He finally agreed and he has been successful voicing his commercials ever since.

Many brands have been successfully promoted through sales campaigns built around developing a "relationship" between the company owner/leader and the buying public. What would Kentucky Fried Chicken be without Colonel Sanders? Dave Thomas brought a face and a hometown voice to the experience of having a burger at Wendy's. Lee Iacocca is still remembered more as an extraordinary pitchman for Chrysler than as its CEO. On a local level, you need to be able to objectively determine whether a local owner is adequately "believable" and "relatable" to be featured in company advertisements. If not, the campaign could fall flat.

COMPONENTS OF A SUCCESSFUL COMMERCIAL

While there is no one set formula for creating successful commercials, there are a number of independent elements that need to be considered. It is the combination of these elements that will determine the 7effectiveness of a campaign. Jon Spoelstra, in the book *Marketing Outrageously* suggests that bland marketing is bad marketing. In his words, "Bland doesn't make the buyer think—bland doesn't touch the emotions of buyers—and bland doesn't motivate people to buy." If it's not outstanding, it doesn't stand out.

COPYWRITING

The storyline must capture the attention of the target audience in the first 5 to 7 seconds or the "what's in it for me?" syndrome will probably result in a tune-out (physically or mentally). The hardest part about creating compelling copy is keeping it within the time allotted. Too often, the "central message" is lost while trying to get in product selection, sale prices, location, directions, telephone numbers and a host of other copy points provided. The most effective commercials focus on one central theme—the net takeaway.

Although radio and television are mass media, the most effective campaigns address their target audience as individuals, one person at a time. That's why many commercials use the words "you" and "your" in their spots. If they can get you personally to step into their little world and imagine yourself on the beaches of a resort in Jamaica, they are halfway there. Telling a story is good, but putting the viewer or listener in the story is even better. Phrases such as "Imagine yourself..."

and "Have you ever..." do just that, drawing the audience into the scenario.

Some stations have professional copywriters, whereas others rely on the sales force to create their own ads. Even if you have a copywriter to hand off that phase of the project to, no one knows your clients and their companies as well as you do. If others are creating your ads, make sure that they vividly portray the experience you wish to convey and the goal that you want to achieve. Provide your copywriters with sufficient guidance and information so that they can do a good job for you. A price and item cutout of the newspaper will not do for copy points. Finally, no matter who is generating the ads, make sure they follow all the old copywriting wisdom: Sell the benefits, not the features. Features show the "what"— benefits sell the "why."

VOICING

Choosing the voice to carry the commercial is one of the most important decisions you can make. The total image of a campaign can be changed by this one variable. Would a jewelry store commercial be more relatable and ultimately more effective for your target audience if it were delivered by a female or by a male? Or, if the ad is being written for Mother's Day, how about using the voice of a child describing the joy on her mother's face when she opened the box? The voice(s) should be relevant and appropriate to the market you are trying to reach.

Another issue to consider is: Would the message be more effective being delivered by one person or would a two-person conversation be more compelling? If it is the latter, the more believable the conversation (i.e., speaking the way people really speak), the more effective the commercial. Molson Golden Ale had an extremely successful campaign built around a conversation between a man and woman that almost made you believe that you were eavesdropping on a couple's flirting.

Jim Gentry, Creative Director for the Barber Martin Agency in Richmond, Virginia suggests that copywriters think of the character, the emotion and the sound of the voices you are going for before you commit the copy to paper. Then as you begin to write the script, write it through the voice and mind of that character (or those characters). How would they deliver the words? What inflection and tone would be used? Would the character have a high-energy, rushed delivery or would it be more reserved? Are they exuding sincerity or excitement? Choose the talent that best matches your vision and coach them to achieve your goal.

PRODUCTION VALUE

Is the image of your client's company adequately reflected in the commercial? Do the graphics and pictures present the best of what the company has to offer? Television advertisers should capitalize on the visual advantages the medium offers.

While television production is not cheap, you usually get what you pay for. Too often, production costs are reduced to leave more dollars for the purchase of airtime. While frequency is absolutely needed, showing a poorly produced commercial that does little to "sell" a business, product or service will ultimately do more harm than good. This is not to say that every commercial has to be an elaborate production. It's just that on a tight budget, money spent on being a little more compelling in the copy and a little more creative in the layout usually pays off.

SOUND DESIGN

The creative concept for radio is built on the auditory equivalent of a blank piece of canvas. The copywriter's words coupled with the producer's sound effects should paint sound images in the "theater of the mind." Just as the old-time radio programs told stories that captured the imagination, generating vivid pictures in listeners' minds, modern-day radio commercials can do the same. A commercial should help create an image of the advertiser in the listeners' minds even before they have ever been to the place of business or experienced what is being sold. Imagine yourself lying on the sands in Jamaica, the hot sun warming your skin, the sounds of waves crashing, seagulls calling and a reggae band jamming in the background. These images can easily be created in a radio spot—and very cost effectively as well. The sounds will conjure up emotional images that are unique and personal for each listener. If effective, this is a classic case of appealing to the heart (desire)—and the mind will follow.

SOUNDTRACK

The Academy Awards include an Oscar for the "Best Original Soundtrack." I once watched a segment of the televised awards show in which they demonstrated what clips of the movies would look like without the music to carry the scenes. It is not until you hear (or, rather, don't hear) the difference that you realize how much music creates the mood and enhances the audience's emotional reaction during movie scenes.

The same is true in commercial production. Even if you use the same copy and the same voice, altering or eliminating the music that carries the commercial totally changes the feeling that is generated. You should always be aware of what mood you are trying to create. For a series of jewelry tips, would a new-age guitar background work better than a light jazz piano carry? If you are selling diamond rings to a young male buyer, a different background might be more appropriate. The soundtrack must be relevant to, and must resonate with, your target market.

Music can be used to transport the imagination to a different place and time. It can also accentuate humor and add depth to a character. In addition, research proves that music can make your commercial more memorable. After a commercial is heard a few times, just hearing the beginning of the soundtrack can trigger associated images in a listener's mind.

Come on Baby Light My Fire
-The Doors

18. HOW TO PRESENT TO THE CLIENT

THE PRESENTATION

Ask a dozen different sales trainers the best format for a presentation, and you'll most likely get a dozen different answers. Some trainers favor a multi-page analysis with a list of recommendations. Others suggest no more than a one-page proposal. The Radio Advertising Bureau (RAB) has a recommended proposal format, and many broadcast groups or individual markets within these groups have tried to standardize their format of choice.

While this "one size fits all" presentation format works well for some groups, the challenge is that it is often difficult to standardize a presentation format that works well for everyone. To begin with, different salespeople have different levels of talent, knowledge and expertise when it comes to creating in-depth marketing presentations. In addition, different clients have different levels of marketing sophistication and different personality profiles (see earlier chapter), which should be taken into account when preparing the presentation. Every sales opportunity is a unique situation, bringing together at least two unique personalities. Work with your manager to identify a format that is right for you.

Regardless of the format, the most critical check points

going into a presentation are: (1) that you have put a lot of thought into the analysis of the client's business, (2) that you have generated well-thought-out recommendations to help the client solve a problem or to create opportunities for growth and (3) that these recommendations are well communicated.

The reality is that if all the other elements discussed in this book are covered leading up to the presentation, getting agreement on the presentation should be the easy part. Rarely can you go wrong by doing too much research, offering too in-depth an analysis or by making too many marketing suggestions. A cookie-cutter schedule with an added value promotion will not differentiate you from your competition. If you can come up with new ways to affect the "triggers" of the client's business, your value as a marketing resource will be solidified.

The presentation should be the foundation
that ties the total marketing campaign together.

HELP THEIR BUSINESS GROW – YOUR BUSINESS WILL FOLLOW

What is the end result of all of your hard work? What happens when you go the extra mile to make sure that your clients' campaigns are successful? When a campaign is a success, your client's business is increased. When your client's business is increased, their advertising budget grows. When their advertising budget grows, they will be loyal to the one that helped them along the way. Consequently, your business will grow as well. As you grow the number of clients that you help each year, your business grows exponentially. As the number of your successful campaigns grows, so does your confidence. As your confidence grows, so does your stature and reputation in the field. As your reputation grows, your referral base grows.... and so on.

Be a student of the industry until you feel you know it. Then be a graduate student of the industry and continue to learn more—and don't forget the post-graduate studies. You'll find that what you've always heard is true: Success breeds success.

**Life is a journey, not a destination.
Enjoy the journey!**

BIBLIOGRAPHY

There are many great business books that share research, stories and advice on how to improve your sales and marketing efforts. The following are ones that have inspired me with useful information that I share in this book, and are therefore, recommended for further reading.

Beckwith, Harry. *What Clients Love: A Field Guide to Growing Your Business.* New York: Warner Books, 2003.

Carlson, Richard. *Don't Sweat the Small Stuff...And it's All Small Stuff.* New York: Hyperion, 1997.

Collins, James C. and Porras, Jerry I. *Built to Last: Successful Habits of Visionary Companies.* New York: Harper Collins, 1994.

Collins, Jim. *Good to Great.* New York: Harper Collins, 2001.

Corbett, Michael. *The 33 Ruthless Rules of Local Advertising.* New York: Pinnacle Books, 2002.

Covey, Stephen R. *The 7 Habits of Highly Effective People: Powerful Lessons in Personal Change.* New York: Simon and Schuster, 1989.

Gladwell, Malcolm. *The Tipping Point: How Little Things Can Make a Big Difference.* Boston: Little, Brown and Company, 2000.

Ogilvy, David. *Ogilvy on Advertising.* New York: Vintage Books, 1983.

Papazian, Ed. *TV Dimensions 2005.* New York: Media Dynamics, 2005.

Roberts, Kevin. *Lovemarks: The Future Beyond Brands.* New York: Powerhouse Books, 2004.

Spoelstra, Jon. *Marketing Outrageously: How to Increase Your*

Revenue by Staggering Amounts. Atlanta: Bard Press, 2001.

Spector, Robert. *The Nordstrom Way: The Inside Story of America's #1 Customer Service Company.* New York: John Wiley & Sons Inc., 1995.

Taylor, Don. *Up Against The Wal-Marts: How Your Business Can Prosper in the Shadow of the Retail Giants.* Saranac Lake, New York: Amacom, 1996.

Williams, Roy. *The Wizard of Ads: Turning Words into Magic and Dreamers into Millionaires.* Austin: Bard Press, 1998.

Williams, Roy. *Secret Formulas of the Wizard of Ads.* Austin: Bard Press, 1999.

Williams, Roy. *Magical Worlds of the Wizard of Ads: Tools and Techniques for Profitable Persuasion.* Austin: Bard Press, 2001.

Winston, Stephanie. *The Organized Executive.* New York: Fireside, 1995.